Marin County Bike Trails

*Easy to Challenging Bicycle Rides
for Touring and Mountain Bikes*

by
Phyllis L. Neumann
Author of *Sonoma County Bike Trails*

Illustrations by Mary H. Dicke

D0950937

PENNGROVE PUBLICATIONS
50 Crest Way
Penngrove, CA 94951
(707) 795-8911

To my husband, Bob,
in loving appreciation,
for his encouragement and support,
as well as his help in producing this book.

Library of Congress Catalog Card Number 88-63918
International Standard Book Number 0-9621694-0-4

Cover photography by Jeff Dooley.
Panoramic Highway on the west slope of Mt. Tamalpais State Park,
overlooking Stinson Beach.

Printed in the United States of America.

Lithocraft, Inc.
947 Piner Place
Santa Rosa, California

First printing, April 1989

PENNGROVE PUBLICATIONS
50 Crest Way
Penngrove, CA 94951
(707) 795-8911

TABLE OF CONTENTS

ACKNOWLEDGMENTS

All books need the help of good friends and family to stimulate and encourage such a large undertaking. I could not have written this book without it. Therefore, in warmest appreciation, I wish to thank:

- *Rawls Frazier,* who scoped out many of the rides and acted as a major consultant and editor for the manuscript. My deepest appreciation.

- *Jim Platt,* who wrote several of the mountain bike rides and who also graciously edited the manuscript. Thanks, Jim.

- *Jeff Dooley,* who photographed the cover and took several other beautiful photographs. Jeff also contributed information about several rides and wrote *Annual Bicycling Events.*

- *Cindy Neumann,* my lovely daughter, who rode a couple of the rides, took some excellent photographs and helped to edit the manuscript.

- *Warren Long,* of Lithocraft, Inc., who not only helped me produce a professional quality book but, because of his expertise, made the production of this book flow smoothly. Thanks for being there, Warren.

BICYCLE TRAILS COUNCIL OF MARIN

The *Bicycle Trails Council of Marin* is an organization of over 300 bikers and hikers who have come together out of a love for bicycling and a concern for the environment in which they practice their sport. The BTC was formed in 1987 by Dave Garoutte, a native of Mill Valley, to represent safe, responsible off-road cycling with an environmental orientation. For more information contact:

Bicycle Trails Council of Marin
P.O. Box 13842
San Rafael, CA 94913-3842
(415) 472-BIKE

EXPLORE MARIN COUNTY BY BIKE!

Marin County is one of the most beautiful areas in California. Surrounded on three sides by water, Marin extends north from the Golden Gate Bridge, west to the coast, east to San Pablo Bay, with majestic Mount Tamalpais towering right in the center at 2,571 feet. The county features a combination of spectacular views, rugged cliffs, natural beaches, well-developed parks, rural farmlands and tiny hidden towns. Marin has it all — exquisite natural beauty combined with sophisticated elegance.

Marin is an area of diversity, changing from luxury to rural within half an hour — from the quick pace of tourist towns to the quiet charm of the country, from the majestic mountain ridges of Mt. Tamalpais and the Marin Headlands to picturesque beach coves, from the redwoods of Muir Woods to the lakes of the Marin Municipal Water District. For an area just north of San Francisco it is surprising that there are such large stretches of almost uninhabited land, complete with wildlife and many varieties of birds of prey.

Marin is a mixture of artistic towns like Sausalito, busy cities like San Rafael, and tiny, remote villages like Inverness and Point Reyes Station. Even its climate is diverse, changing dramatically from sunny to foggy within a few miles — and sometimes within a few minutes. The main population of Marin stretches along Highway 101, which cuts longitudinally through the eastern edge of the county. The further west you travel the more rural it becomes.

Bicycling in Marin is always exciting because the elevation changes so dramatically from place to place. Some rides will take some strenuous pedaling to appreciate the magnificent views; other rides are flat and easy, perfect for families with small children. Approximately one-third of the county's land has been reserved for parks and preserves, giving you the opportunity to ride along beaches and mountain ridges that are protected from cars. Designated bike paths are found in most towns. Because of its mild seasons biking in Marin is a favorite activity any time of the year.

Marin County Bike Trails has been written with the casual cyclist in mind — the person or family that wants to take advantage of what Marin County has offer. Marin is waiting for you to explore her. Once you get on your bike here you'll never want to get off!

MARIN COUNTY MAP

REGIONS OF MARIN COUNTY

SOUTHERN MARIN

The Golden Gate Bridge marks the entrance to southern Marin County. Here you can enjoy picture-postcard vistas of San Francisco and the Bay, where sailboats drift silently by. Droves of tourists come to the towns of Sausalito and Tiburon each weekend to take in the magnificent views, quaint shops, fabulous restaurants, and incredible scenery. Bicycle rides in this region vary from being almost flat in the city areas to steep grades on mountain ridges overlooking the Pacific.

CENTRAL MARIN

This central part of Marin boasts of rugged mountains, majestic redwood forests and sweeping vistas. Much of it has been preserved for Mt. Tamalpais and the Marin Municipal Water District, which includes five lovely reservoirs. Bicycle riding here can entail some moderate to steep grades, many of them leading to the summit of Mt. Tamalpais. Because of the preservation of the area this is an excellent place for taking your mountain bike.

WEST MARIN

The magnifient California coastline awaits you. Here you can climb to the highest cliffs for incredible views of the Pacific. Tiny, remote villages like Bolinas and Stinson Beach line the southern end of the Marin Coast. Farther north along the coast, in Inverness, Olema, Point Reyes Station life is slow and peaceful and relatively unchanged. These tiny communities along the coast seem to be shielded by time. Many of the bike trails in this area can get fairly steep, but this is also one of the most picturesque parts of the county. The climate can get quite foggy and windy here, so always carry a jacket with you.

NORTH MARIN

This part of the county takes you deep into Marin farmlands. This area has a rural country setting, with peaceful country roads and gentle rolling hills. The area is dotted with large horse and cattle ranches and dairy farms. Because it is less populated here, traffic is generally light. Bicycle trails are gentler and easier to ride with excellent paved roads.

TIPS FOR BETTER TOURING

The way people take a bike trip covers a wide range of needs and speeds, depending upon individual capabilities, equipment, weather conditions, terrain, or just how you feel that day and who you're with. All bicyclists have individual needs, depending upon their riding styles, degrees of experience, and personalities. A beginner cannot keep pace with an experienced cyclist, and therefore shouldn't try. Choosing gentle grades and taking frequent rests ensure an enjoyable introduction to cycling.

How can you improve your riding efficiency? Experienced cyclists develop a rhythm and pedal at a relatively constant rate of speed. This is called cadence and is measured in crank revolutions per minute (rpm). Each individual has a natural cadence which he feels most comfortable for him or her. Casual cyclists seem to develop a cadence rate between 55-75 rpm, whereas racing cyclists establish a cadence somewhere between 90-100 rpm. Beginners often tend to pedal too slowly. Count your pedal strokes per minute. If your rate is much below 60 rpm, try pedaling faster by switching to a lower gear to maintain a good average pace.

The most common mistake beginners make is to start off with a burst of speed in the morning and then burn out before noon. It is more efficient to keep up a steady rhythm, mile after mile, uphill or down, rather than to use the "pedal-coast" style of riding. The body works best when it builds up stamina evenly and gradually instead of in short spurts.

The gears on a touring or mountain bike permit you to maintain your most efficient natural cadence, regardless of most terrain. When pedaling becomes too easy and there is little pedal resistance, shift to a higher gear; when it gets too difficult to maintain cadence, shift to a lower gear. Of course, there are times when nothing helps. Those are the time to get off and hike it!

A note of interest for you calorie-counters: Moderate cycling uses up an average of 5 calories per minute, or 300 calories per hour. Vigorous cycling, the kind you do going up a hill, uses up approximately 10 calories per minute, or 600 calories per hour. There are 3500 calories in one pound.

HOW TO USE THIS BOOK

This book is written for people who enjoy rides where the touring is just as important as the pedaling. There are short, easy rides for beginners or families with small children, as well as challenging rides for those out for a day's adventure.

The riding time specified in the book is to be used only as a flexible guide, not taking into account rest stops or sightseeing. In general, you can estimate your own riding time as follows:

5-10 miles per hour	beginning or inexperienced riders traveling at a casual, leisurely pace
10-20 miles per hour	good, strong riders traveling at a moderate pace
20-30 miles per hour	serious cyclists in good condition traveling at a steady, brisk pace

The rides either return on the same road or are loop trips, ending at the same place they begin without retracing their path. They have been rated as *easy, medium,* or *challenging*.

An *easy* ride is one that is relatively short (10 miles or less), has easy or no grades, and can be ridden by beginners and children.

A *medium* ride is a bit longer (10-20 miles), and may include some moderate grades, though none too strenuous or too steep.

A *challenging* ride is for experienced riders (or ambitious ones), and measures 20 miles or longer, taking several hours to half a day to complete. It will exhaust the beginner. The grades can be relatively steep and there may be several of them.

Variations of the rides describe other routes that may be used instead of, or in addition to, the original ride. They are noted at the end of each ride and are also indicated on the map by broken lines.

Alternate rides may be used in place of the original ride. They are noted at the end of each ride and are also listed on page 99.

Maps of the ride indicate the route to be ridden in strong, bold lines, while the adjoining roads are marked in lighter lines. Variations and extensions of the ride are indicated by broken lines. The arrow shows you where to begin and in which direction.

Elevation Profiles of the rides were recorded at ½-mile intervals and are invaluable in giving a graphic picture of the terrain, and will help you to determine whether the trip is more (or less) difficult than you want to tackle that day.

SOUTH MARIN

1. Crossing The
GOLDEN GATE BRIDGE

Region: *South Marin* **Rating:** *Easy*
Mileage: *4 miles* **Riding Time:** *1 hour or less*
Type of Bike: *Mountain or Touring Bike*

Terrain: *Protected paved bike lane. The ride is relatively flat although the bridge has a natural curve across the span.*

Starting Location/Parking: *Traveling south on Hwy 101 take the Marin Headlands exit to the West Walkway parking lot by the north tower of the Golden Gate Bridge. From Hwy 101 north, take the Alexander Avenue exit and go under the freeway. Park your car at the West Walkway parking lot.*

Description of Ride: *One of the most exciting bicycling thrills has to be riding across the Golden Gate Bridge. The magnificent views of San Francisco to the south, the rugged Marin hills to the north, and San Francisco Bay below make this a unique bicycling experience — much more than you would ever see by car. The views are awesome!*

The Golden Gate Bridge is the gateway to both San Francisco and Marin County. It is undoubtedly one of the most beautiful bridges in the world because of its spectacular location, its graceful lines and unusual bright orange/red color. It was a bridge that was thought could never be built. Joseph Strauss, its chief engineer, proved them wrong in an incredible engineering feat, taking only 4½ years and costing less than originally estimated. The bridge's 4,200-foot span is one of the longest in the world, is designed to withstand 100 mile-an-hour winds and able to swing at mid-span as much as 27 feet.

WEST SIDEWALK (Weekends Only)

The west sidewalk is reserved for cyclists on weekends, away from the tourist foot traffic on the East Sidewalk. Riding across the bridge was once prohibited; now hundreds of bicyclists of all ages can be seen riding across the bridge to and from San Francisco. All walkways on the bridge close at sunset, therefore be sure that you plan enough time to get back over the bridge before then.

WEST SIDEWALK ENTRANCE

Weekends and holidays: open 5:00 a.m. — 9:00 p.m.
Weekdays: open 3:30 p.m. – 9:00 p.m.

Bicyclists only — No pedestrians

Riding over the Golden Gate Bridge

Photo: Jeff Dooley

EAST SIDEWALK (Weekdays)

The bridge is continuously being repainted. It seems to be a never-ending task because, as soon as they complete it, they start all over again. During weekdays the bridge maintenance crews use the west walkway for their equipment, thus bicyclists must use the east walkway to cross the bridge.

Begin your ride at the Vista Point parking lot at the north end of the Golden Gate Bridge. Here you will find a sweeping panoramic view of the San Francisco Bay. Don't forget your camera! There is no access to Vista Point if you are traveling south on Highway 101. However, you always have the option of driving across the Bridge, paying your $2.00, and returning to Vista Point. The new gardens commemorate the 50th anniversary of the opening of the bridge in 1937.

Variation: Sausalito to the Golden Gate Bridge

Getting to the Golden Gate Bridge from Sausalito takes some effort. The long uphill grade from Sausalito is gentle but may be somewhat strenuous for beginners. Follow Bridgeway south from Sausalito along the water until it makes a sharp right turn. The road follows the Bay, winding through residential areas and curving up out of the city toward Hwy 101. The road turns into Richardson. The Bay overlook is spectacular. Take an immediate left onto Second Street and up the hill. You will pass The Chart House (Valhalla), which used to be Sally Stanford's famous restaurant. Turn left onto South Street and continue to climb. At the top of the hill, the road turns to the right and becomes Alexander Drive.

West Sidewalk. Turn left onto East Road into the U.S. Army Reserve Center (Fort Baker). Watch for traffic when making your left turn! Wind downhill through the parade grounds, past the public fishing pier, and ultimately go underneath the Golden Gate Bridge. This is an angle you rarely see of the Bridge. Continue uphill to the west side of the bridge and the West Sidewalk.

East Sidewalk. Cut over to the left side of the road, steering away from the underpass. Follow the freeway off-ramp to the left. You're moving against oncoming traffic for a short distance, but there's plenty of room on the paved shoulder for safe passage. Turn into the Vista Point parking lot where you'll find the way to the East Sidewalk of the Golden Gate Bridge.

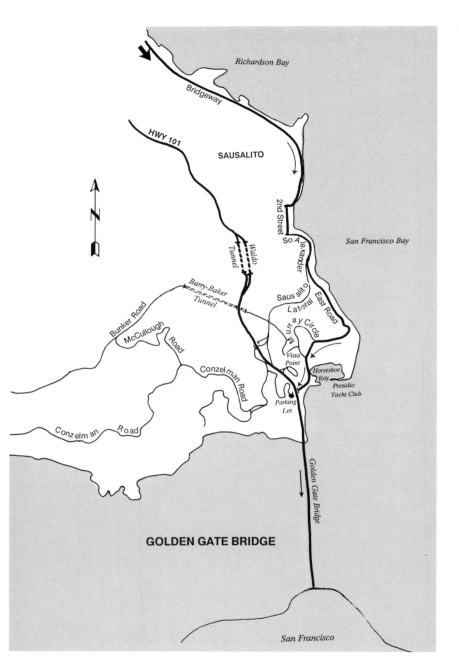

Richardson Bay

Bridgeway

HWY 101

SAUSALITO

N

2nd Street

So Alexander

San Francisco Bay

Waldo Tunnel

Barry-Baker Tunnel

Bunker Road

McCullough Road

Sausalito Lateral

East Road

Murray Circle

Conzelman Road

Vista Point

Horseshoe Bay

Presidio Yacht Club

Parking Lot

Conzelman Road

Golden Gate Bridge

GOLDEN GATE BRIDGE

San Francisco

2. SAUSALITO
Mill Valley to Sausalito

Region: *South Marin*   **Rating:** *Easy*
Mileage: *8½ miles*   **Riding Time:** *1 hour*
Type of Bike: *Touring or Mountain Bike*

Terrain: *Flat, paved bike path*

Description: *This is an easy, flat ride for the whole family to enjoy. A beautiful, paved bike path that shares the road only with other bicycles, joggers and walkers, takes you from the outskirts of Mill Valley to downtown Sausalito where you can view the magnificence of San Francisco Bay. On weekends there is heavy traffic, but the bike path avoids most of it. The route can be a bit confusing and you will need to pay attention to the map to get to the back roads and avoid the traffic.*

Starting Location/Parking: *Begin your ride at Bayfront Park in Mill Valley. Take Hwy 101 to the East Blithedale exit. Turn left on Camino Alto to Sycamore Avenue. Turn left on Sycamore to Bayfront Park.*

Route: *From Bayfront Park follow the bike path south towards the freeway, across Bothin Marsh. Continue for two miles as the bike path parallels Bridgeway. At Harbor Drive turn left and then a quick right onto Marinship Way, and follow the sign pointing to the Bay Model. At Napa Road pick up the bike path again and take it to Johnson Street. Turn left and follow the Bike Route sign through the back parking lots to Garrielson Park. Return to Bayfront Park along the same route.*

Begin your ride at Bayfront Park, along a lovely wide bike path that has been built on an old railroad levee. You will be sharing this wide, flat road with other cyclists, joggers and walkers, so stay to your right. The path parallels Camino Alto on the right and Bothin Marsh on the left, with a view of the freeway overpass crossing the tip of Richardson Bay.

After about a mile the bike path begins to veer away from Camino Alto and head toward the freeway underpass. Once you pass under the freeway you parallel Highway 101 for a bit. The ambience changes dramatically as the roar of traffic from the nearby freeway fills your ears. If you look back to the north you can see majestic Mt. Tamalpais looking down from its summit.

On your left you will pass Seaplane/Helicopter rides. Directly across the freeway is the large Marin Flea Market, which is open on weekends. If you wish to see it cross Bridgeway at the intersection of Gate 6 Road. There is no admission and always loads of souvenirs and food to buy. Also at the corner of Gate 6 Road is a small shopping center, *Harbor Center, Sausalito.* Here the bike path divides with large round wood posts separating walkers from bicyclists. The bike lane is on the left side. At Harbor Drive turn left and then a quick right onto Marinship Way. This back road is flat with no traffic and parallels Bridgeway for a while, eliminating the hill on Bridgeway while letting you explore boat shops and boat yards, as well as the large marinas.

At the stop sign on Marinship Way turn right at the sign saying *Bay Model.* Small Marinship Park has restrooms and tennis courts.

The San Francisco Bay Delta Model is a hydraulic working scale model of the entire San Francisco Bay and Delta. It is used by engineers and scientists to analyze the Bay's characteristics and behavior with regard to tidal action, water currents, fresh and salt water mixing, and sediment movement. The Model is approximately 1½ acres in size and is open to the public Tuesday through Friday,

View of Angel Island from Garrielson Park   Photo: Phyllis Neumann

from 10 a.m. to 4 p.m., and on Saturday, from 9 a.m. to 4 p.m. Admission is free.

From the Model keep to your left onto a paved bike path which continues through the back parking lot of an office building. At the stop sign on Napa Road is *Earl F. Dunphy Park,* a small, lovely and uncrowded park that sits on Richardson Bay, looking lazily out on the sailboats passing by. A small gazebo stands off to the side of it. You might consider picnicking here since it is usually not crowded.

When you leave the park return to the divided bike path on Bridgeway. On the weekend this street can become quite congested. The bike path ends abruptly at Johnson Street. Here turn left and then a quick right to follow the *Bike Route* sign through several back parking lots. Be careful of people in parked cars who may not see you and open their car door suddenly. These parking lots will lead you to Garrielson Park, another lovely park.

Garrielson Park overlooks Richardson Bay and the entrance to Raccoon Strait. In the distance you can see the Bay Bridge and the Richmond/Berkeley hills. Sailboats cruise quietly by. On a clear day this spot is truly the essence of what Marin County is all about.

The town of Sausalito was originally named *Saucelito* in 1775 by a Spanish explorer, and means "little willow," for the willows growing near a hillside spring. By the turn of the century Sausalito had become a retreat for artists, writers and brothels. One of the city's most famous madames was Sally Stanford, who, in her later years opened and ran Valhalla, an elegant restaurant on the south end of town. In 1976, amid considerable national publicity, she was elected major of Sausalito. Today Sausalito is a major tourist attraction as well as a National Historical Landmark District offering tourists unique art galleries, sophisticated shops, elegant waterfront restaurants and several picturesque, peaceful parks. Ferry service is available daily to and from San Francisco.

Continue on a bit further, past the Sausalito Yacht Club (SYC Building) and you will find another magnificent vista of the San Francisco Bay. Bike racks are strategically placed so that you can browse through Sausalito without worrying about your bike. If these are filled, as they tend to be on weekends, there are more available in Garrielson Park.

Variation: Crossing the Golden Gate Bridge (Easy — 4 miles). You might want to combine this ride with Ride No. 1.

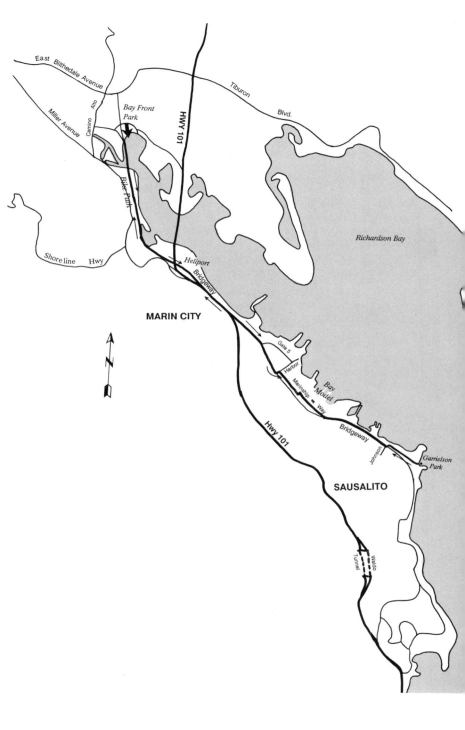

3. MARIN HEADLANDS
Golden Gate National Recreation Area

Region: *South Marin*　　　　　**Rating:** *Challenging*
Mileage: *9½ miles*　　　　　　**Riding Time:** *1-2 hours*
Type of Bike: *Mountain or Touring Bike*

Terrain: *Paved road with several steep grades. Little traffic.*

Description of Ride: *This ride, although fairly steep in some areas, has some of the most spectacular scenery in Marin County. You climb up rugged cliffs along the Pacific Ocean. Some of the best views of San Francisco and the Pacific are seen from the bluffs of the Headlands. The weather can quickly become quite windy and foggy, so always carry a jacket with you.*

Starting Location/Parking: *From Highway 101 going south take the Sausalito exit, turn left to the Marin Headlands to Conzelman Road. From Highway 101 going north take the Alexander Avenue (Sausalito) Exit, wind downhill and go under the Golden Gate Bridge and follow Conzelman Road. Park your car off the road at the small junction of McCullough and Conzelman Roads.*

Route: *From the junction of McCullough and Conzelman Roads take Conzelman up the steep climb and continue past the One-Way sign down the hill and along the cliffs. Take Field Road to Bunker Road. Turn left on Bunker Road to Rodeo Lagoon and the Visitors Center. Return on Bunker Road, turn right onto McCullough Road until you reach the junction McCullough and Conzelman Roads and your car.*

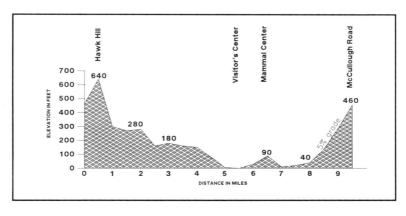

Marin Headlands is a contrast of awesome natural beauty and remnants of military bunkers. Three forts exist on the land: Forts Baker, Cronkhite, and Barry. At Fort Baker, on the east side of the bridge, about 100 servicemen are still stationed there.

In 1972 the Marin Headlands became part of the Golden Gate National Recreation Area (GGNRA) which includes 40,000 acres in Marin County alone, thus protecting the land from further development. There is a visitor's center in Fort Cronkhite where you can get maps and information about the Headlands. Whenever you go, always bring along a sweater or jacket. Even on the warmest days it can become quite chilly out here and the weather can change quite suddenly.

To begin your ride park your car at the small junction of McCullough and Conzelman Roads. The ride starts with a steep climb for about a half-mile. At the lookout point the road becomes one-way for cars. You can climb to the top of Battery Hill 129, nicknamed "Hawk Hill," and see the Bay Area and San Francisco skyline from its highest point at the lookout. It's really spectacular from here. This is where many photographs and posters are taken of the Golden Gate Bridge.

From this point it's all downhill — and what a ride it is! You begin coasting down curving mountain cliffs with incredibly

View from the top of Hawk Hill

breathtaking views all around you. Keep your eyes on the road through this steep and winding route, although it's hard to do because it is so incredibly beautiful.

You can get a glimpse of the Pt. Bonita Lighthouse on your left, with its beacon blinking rhythmically. The Lighthouse is open seasonally on weekends. The road is smooth with few cars and a joy to ride. It begins to climb again. If you look down to your right you can see the Presidio Riding Stable below. You will pass boarded up ammunition bunkers. From the ridge you can get some incredible views of the coast, the lighthouse, and the buildings of Fort Cronkhite.

At the junction you will see signs to the beach to the right or Point Bonita Lighthouse to the left. At the intersection turn left and take the 1½-mile loop to the left to see the lighthouse and explore the bunkers. Field Road will eventually return you to this point.

Continue on down the hill on Field Road toward Rodeo Lagoon and the beach area. At Bunker Road turn left and follow the road to the beach. Here you can visit the Marin Headlands Visitor Center, the Golden Gate Youth Hostel, the Art Center. On the way back plan to stop at the Mammal Rehabilitation Center.

The road is flat and easy. The flag pole marks the Marin Headlands Visitor Center, where you can get maps and books of the area. Just past the Visitor Center is Rodeo Beach, where you can find picnic tables, water and restrooms — a great place for lunch.

On your return stop at the Marine Mammal Rehabilitation Center. Backtrack to Bunker Road. At the stop sign turn left for your trip back. The road follows the valley and is wide, smooth and flat. At the triangle of Field Road and Bunker Road keep to the left on Field Road. This road is also flat and level here. You stay in the valley for a while. You will pass Presidio Riding Stable on your right. The road begins to rise gradually. Turn right on McCullough Road which begins to climb almost immediately. *Do not go past McCullough Road. Bicycles are prohibited from entering the tunnel.* It is a steep climb and winds around the mountain and back to your car.

Alternate Ride 3a: Bunker Road to Rodeo Lagoon (Easy — 6 miles). For a short, pleasant and easy ride to Rodeo Lagoon and back along Bunker Road. Start at the junction of McCullough and Bunker Roads and take Bunker Road to Rodeo Lagoon and the Visitor Center. Have a picnic lunch, tour the Mammal Center and return to your car.

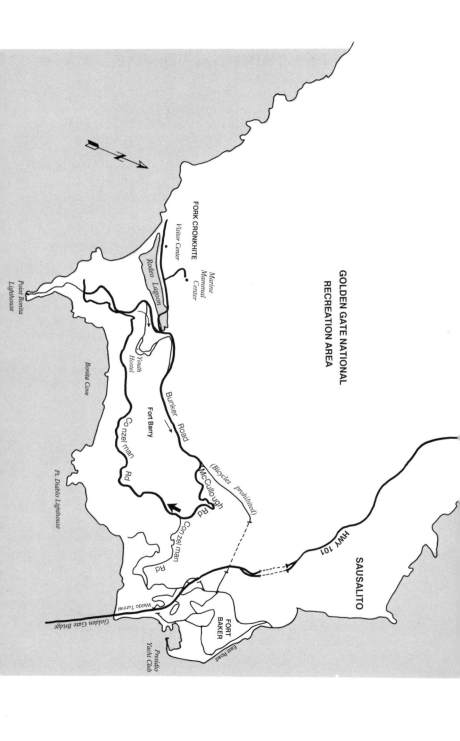

4. TIBURON PENINSULA

Region: *South Marin*   **Rating:** *Medium*
Mileage: *9 miles*   **Riding Time:** *1-2 hours*
Type of Bike: *Touring or Mountain Bike*

Terrain: *Paved bike road to Tiburon. Moderate climbs around peninsular.*

Description: *A flat, easy ride to the town of Tiburon. A more difficult ride around the Peninsula, with some moderate climbs. This ride is one of the most popular in Marin.*

Starting Location/Parking: *From Hwy 101 take the Tiburon/Belvedere exit (Hwy 131). Follow Tiburon Blvd. east 1½-miles to Blackie's Pasture at the junction of Tiburon Blvd. and Trestle Glen Road.*

Route: *From Blackie's Pasture follow the bike path to the town of Tiburon. Continue on Paradise Drive around the Peninsula for 5 miles until you reach the stop sign at Trestle Glen Road. Take a left back down to Tiburon Blvd. Cross the street back to Blackie's Pasture.*

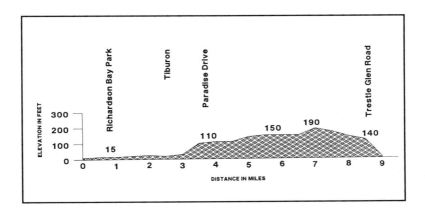

Blackie's Pasture is a large dirt parking lot usually packed with cars on the weekends. Originally it was a pasture where an old, swayback horse named Blackie was kept. He grew to become a favorite of the area and, when he died in 1966, at the age of 33, a picket-fenced grave site, complete with headstone, was placed there in his memory.

At the edge of the parking lot is a well-marked paved bike path in Richardson Bay Lineal Park which leads to downtown Tiburon. The bike path is heavily used by bicyclists, joggers and walkers on the weekends, so ride carefully. It follows the Bay through grassy playing fields, a playground, and parcourse. The bike path eventually joins Tiburon Blvd.

The picturesque town of *Tiburon* means "shark" in Spanish, and has long been a favorite spot to spend a few glorious hours eating at elegant waterfront restaurants and wandering around the quaint little shops and art galleries on Tiburon's Main Street. From here you can also considering taking a short ferry ride to Angel Island, where you can explore the island by bike (see Variation #3).

Just past Main Street is Shoreline Park, an inviting large grassy area where you relax for a while in the sunshine, and listen to the water slapping against the rocks. From this lovely inlet you can watch the sailboats move gracefully by against a backdrop of the magnificent San Francisco skyline.

From Shoreline Park continue your ride. Paradise Drive is aptly named, for the road changes dramatically from a flat city street to a winding, narrow, moderately hilly and picturesque road through the

Shoreline Park in Tiburon

Photo: Cindy Neumann

countryside. Prepare yourself for great panoramic views of the entire Bay Area and a delightful adventure into the country. You will pass *Elephant Rock*, a large boulder surrounded by a small fishing pier and dedicated to children who love to fish.

The road immediately begins to climb out of town. The bike path disappears, and so does the traffic. As you climb you can immediately get a breathtaking glimpse of Raccoon Strait, as hundreds of beautiful sailboats pass before you. Ayala Cove, a small inlet on Angel Island, can be seen right across the Strait. This is where ferries and private boats dock.

You might consider taking a break at *Paradise Beach Park*. The park overlooks the East Bay hills and San Pablo Bay and has a fishing pier, bathroom facilities, water, and picnic tables. It is generally foggy until noon; however, if it is warm enough you may consider a swim. There is a $1 fee.

When the trees become less dense and more shrubs appear you start your descent back down to the parking lot. Turn left at Trestle Glen Road (at the Fire Station) to return to the parking lot. At the stop light cross Tiburon Blvd., ride across the little bridge back to Blackie's pasture and your car.

Variation #1: Belvedere Extension (Medium — 3 miles). This route winds around the Belvedere Peninsula, taking you past some of the most exclusive homes in Marin County. From Tiburon Blvd. turn right onto San Rafael Avenue and follow it to West Shore Road. Turn right on Golden Gate Avenue and climb the hill to the top. Bear right. The road eventually becomes Beach Road which parallels Tiburon Blvd. and brings you into Tiburon through the back route.

Variation #2: Tiburon to Corte Madera (Medium — 9 miles). Continue on Paradise Drive instead of turning on Trestle Glen for an extension of the ride, which will bring you down to Corte Madera. At the Nordstrom Shopping Center turn left and go over the Freeway. This will bring you to Tamalpais Drive. At the second light turn left onto Casa Buena Road, the frontage road which parallels the freeway back to the Tiburon exit. There are some fairly steep hills, but the road is fairly well protected from many cars. Turn left on Plaza, then left on Tower, left on Blithedale and over the freeway onto Tiburon Blvd. Take the bike path on the right to Blackies' Pasture.

Variation #3. Angel Island State Park (Medium — 5 miles). Combine this ride with a trip to Angel Island. The 5¼-mile ride around Angel Island follows the perimeter of the island and is very scenic. The ferry to Angel Island leaves from Main Street in Tiburon every hour on the hour, from 10 a.m. to 5 p.m. every day during the summer and on Saturdays, Sundays, and holidays during the rest of the year, weather permitting. Call ahead to check the schedule.

Variation #4: Mill Valley to Tiburon (Medium — 6½ miles). From Bay Front Park take East Blithedale Avenue to Tiburon Blvd. At the Cove Shopping Center turn right onto the frontage road. There is no congestion on the weekends. Continue the ride as before.

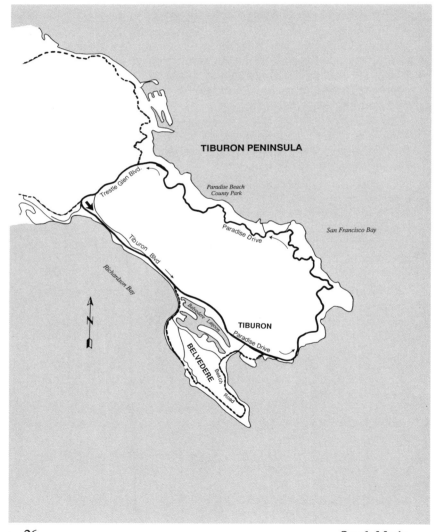

South Marin

5. ANGEL ISLAND STATE PARK

Region: *South Marin*   **Rating:** *Medium*
Mileage: *5¼ Miles*   **Riding Time:** *1 Hour*
Type of Bike: *Touring or Mountain Bike*

Terrain: *Fairly flat with moderate grades. Alternates between paved, dirt and gravel roads. Novice riders may need to walk up a few short but steep hills.*

Description: *Angel Island State Park is one of Marin County's favorite places to take a bike. No book would be complete without including it. Free from motorized traffic, it offers spectacular panoramic views, vista points and picnic areas. The ride will also take you into Angel Island's history, before the island was turned into a state park. Angel Island has some magnificent sights and is definitely a ride for the whole family.*

Starting Location/Parking: *Angel Island is located about one mile from Tiburon on Raccoon Strait. It can only be reached by private boat or ferry, which departs from Main Street in downtown Tiburon or San Francisco. To get to Tiburon take the Tiburon Exit east from Highway 101.*

Route: *From the Visitor's Center take the road to the left up a short steep hill. At the top of the hill turn right and follow Perimeter Road counterclockwise around the circumference of the island.*

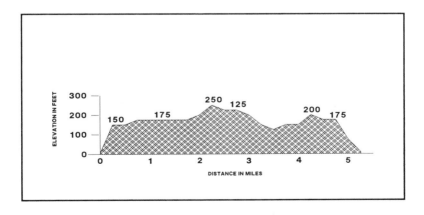

Angel Island has over 740 acres of hiking and biking trails. The most popular main access road, Perimeter Road, circles the island. Most of the other roads on the island are either too rough or too steep for safe or pleasant cycling, though mountain bicycles seem to have little trouble. Some of the trails are restricted to hikers only. Watch for signs.

The island has a colorful history. The first known people to inhabit the island were the Coastal Miwok Indians. Mount Livermore, the highest point on the island (781 feet), was used by the Miwoks as a sacred place. The island was originally covered by dense forest. In 1775, the Spanish explorer, Don Juan Manuel de Ayala, landed on the island and began to cut down the trees for use on his ships. From 1839 to 1850 the island was used as a Mexican cattle ranch by Antonio Mario Osio. From about 1910 to 1940 Angel Island was used as an immigration station, often called the "Ellis Island of the West," to process Asian immigrants entering the United States. During World War II the island was used as a military base and prisoner of war camp for Japanese POWs.

Today Angel Island is a State Park offering hiking, bicycling and picnicking. In the summer a tram can take you around the island on a guided tour. A few beaches can be reached from Perimeter Road, though most of the shoreline has rocky cliffs.

Angel Island Ferry Terminal in Tiburon   Photo: Cindy Neumann

Once you arrive at Ayala Cove by ferry you can pick up maps at the Information Booth. The Snack Bar offers hamburgers, hot dogs and drinks, and bathrooms are located right by the ferry landing. *Ayala Cove* was originally named for Lt. Don Juan Manuel Ayala, captain of the first ship known to sail through the Golden Gate in 1775.

The Visitor Center, behind the lovely grassy picnic grounds, offers a slide presentation of the history of Angel Island on the hour and is well worth seeing. Books, maps and pamphlets about the island are also sold here.

Take the road to the left of the Visitor Center. It immediately turns left up a short, steep hill that may best be walked up. Once you reach the top of the hill the road runs perpendicular in either direction. This ride will follow the island counterclockwise, so turn right at the junction.

Perimeter Road, as the name suggests, encircles the island, and is the best for bicycles, giving you a view of the historic buildings and quarters. The road alternates between paved, dirt, and gravel. Those with touring bikes need to ride more carefully than those with mountain bikes on some parts of the road.

There are vista points along the entire stretch of the ride, strategically placed for viewing the incredible San Francisco Bay and Golden Gate Bridge. Hundreds of beautiful white sails drift quietly past, giving a feeling of serenity.

The road is basically level but includes some substantial grades. If you are a novice or out of condition you will need to get off and walk. Those grades eventually give way to what could be some exciting downhill coasts, but "Walk Your Bike" signs are posted to allow hikers to enjoy the view without danger from careening bicycles.

The entire parameter takes only about an hour to complete but there are several other roads where you can explore other parts of the island, particularly if you have a mountain bike. Bicycles are permitted on most of the trails, however, some of the roads are reserved for hikers.

Angel Island Ferry Schedule. Ferries leave Tiburon from 10 a.m. to 5 p.m. on the hour. The return ferry to Tiburon leaves the island fifteen minutes past the hour and operates until 5:15 p.m. Ferries operate seven days a week from San Francisco and Tiburon during the summer, and weekends only during the off-season. Ferry prices in 1989 were $4.00 for adults plus 50 cents for bicycles.

Variation: Tiburon Peninsula (Medium—9 miles). Link this ride up with a great ride around the Tiburon Peninsula (Ride No. 4).

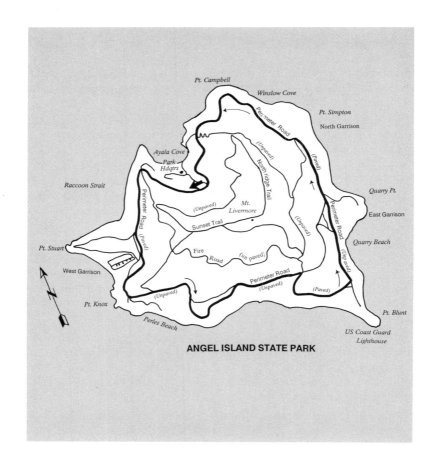

ANGEL ISLAND STATE PARK

CENTRAL MARIN

Mt. Tamalpais

6. MILL VALLEY
Tennessee Valley Trail

Region: *Central Marin*
Mileage: *4 miles*
Type of Bike: *Mountain Bike*

Rating: *Easy*
Riding Time: *1 hour or less*

Terrain: *Wide, dirt fire road with easy grade.*

Description of Ride: *A scenic easy ride through a beautiful valley to a small beach cove. This is one of the most popular rides in the Golden Gate National Recreation area (GGNRA) and is excellent for families with children because no motorized vehicles are permitted. Sunny weekends are usually congested with hikers and equestrians.*

Starting Location/Parking: *From Hwy 101 take the Stinson Beach exit and turn left on Tennessee Valley Road. Drive two miles to the GGNRA entrance gate and parking area.*

Route: *From the gate follow Tennessee Valley Trail to Tennessee Beach, returning the same way.*

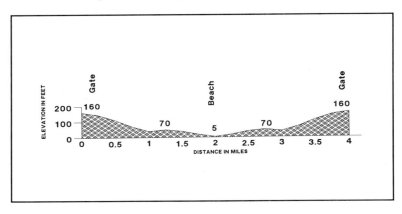

The wooden gate at the end of Tennessee Valley Road marks the entrance to the Marin Headlands. There is a large parking area; however, on nice weekends cars line the road for almost ¼-mile. Miwok Stables is adjacent to the parking lot and provides trail rides through the area.

Once you enter the Marin Headlands you feel immediately removed from the bustle of the city because you are in a beautiful valley flanked by surrounding hills. The paved trail is wide and flat and begins to dip every so slightly, making pedaling almost unnecessary. On weekends ride carefully so as not to interfere with hikers and horses that will be sharing the road with you. The area appears treeless except for patches of brush and a few coastal trees. The trail follows a creek surrounded by a eucalyptus grove with scrub brush, grasslands and chapparral.

After about ¾-mile the pavement ends, turning into a dirt fire road. This trail is also wide and has two short, gentle grades. If you wish to avoid these grades then, at the fork, take the road on the left, which is flat and narrow, and not as firmly packed. If it has recently rained this road could become muddy. The road on the right is firm and remains dry. Both roads lead to Tennessee Beach, so take whichever one suits your mood. Just before you approach the beach you will pass a small lagoon which has a variety of waterfowl.

Tennessee Beach is a small horseshoe cove surrounded by jagged cliffs. It was named after the *SS Tennessee* which ran aground in 1853. There is a bike rack set up on the beach so that you can leave your bike to explore the area or enjoy a picnic by the Pacific. The surf can be dangerous and swimming is not advised.

The two-mile trip to the beach is easy; however, the return trip will use a bit more muscle because it is a mild uphill climb.

Tennessee Valley Road   Photo: Phyllis Neumann

Variations: If you are on a mountain bike you might want to explore the area and other fire roads available to bicycles. Haypress Camp is a secluded primitive campground set in a eucalyptus grove. Several fire roads have steep climbs to the top of the hills where you can get incredible 360° views of San Francisco and Richardson Bays as well as the fantastic San Francisco skyline.

Variation: Tennessee Valley Road to the Gate (Easy – 2 miles). You might wish to start your ride two miles earlier by parking at the north end of Tennessee Valley Road and riding it up to the NNGRA gate. This is a peaceful country road with a mild uphill grade. There's not much weekend traffic along here, and trees line both sides of the road to provide shade on a hot day.

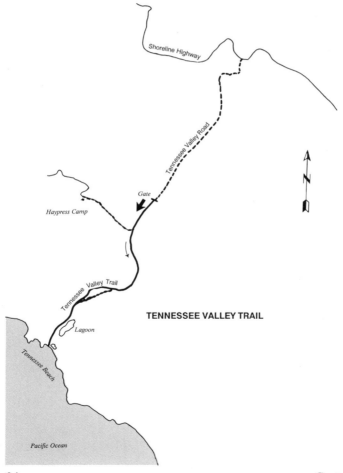

TENNESSEE VALLEY TRAIL

7. MARIN MUNICIPAL WATER DISTRICT
Lake Lagunitas

Region: *Central Marin*
Mileage: *2 miles*
Type of Bike: *Mountain Bike*

Rating: *Easy*
Riding Time: *1 hour or less*

Terrain: *Lovely, gentle, forest trail.*

Description of Ride: *Take your family for a picnic at one of the scenic lakes of the Mt. Tamalpais Watershed. Lake Lagunitas is an easy way to begin because it is a relatively small lake with the circumference of only 2 miles. This is great mountain bike area because there are so many places to explore and miles of side roads that you can take. You can even take your bike all the way to Mt. Tam if you have the stamina to do so.*

Starting Location/Parking: *From Hwy 101 take Sir Francis Drake Blvd. to Fairfax. Turn left onto Bolinas Avenue. Bear left at the wooden sign pointing to Lake Lagunitas. At Sky Oaks Ranger Station there is a $3 day use fee. Follow the road past the east end of Bon Tempe Lake 1¾-miles to the Parking Lot.*

Route: *From the Lake Lagunitas parking lot take the trail to the right of the restrooms up to the dam. Follow the trail counterclockwise around the lake, returning to the parking lot.*

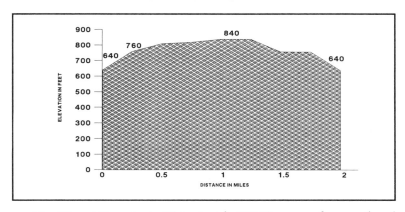

The *Mount Tamalpais Watershed* is 20,000 acres of recreational land, which is administered by the Marin Municipal Water District, and is one of the most beautiful areas in Marin County. The Watershed collects and stores rainwater in five reservoirs: Phoenix,

Bon Tempe, Lagunitas, Alpine and Kent. The area offers fishing, picnic areas, hiking, as well as limited biking and horse paths.

Lake Lagunitas is one of the oldest and smallest of the five lakes in the Marin Municipal Water District. The area around Lake Lagunitas and Bon Tempe Lakes are not crowded, even on weekends, though you'll be sharing the trails with hikers and equestrians, so be alert for them.

The Sky Oaks Ranger Station is at the top of the ridge leading to Mt. Tamalpais and, because you are at 700-foot elevation, your views are always great. You may prefer to park your car at the ranger station and explore that area, riding your bike 1¾-miles up the steep grade to Lake Lagunitas.

Begin your ride at the parking lot which is several miles from the Ranger Station. Park your car here and take the trail adjacent to the restrooms. You will climb a bit to the dam but this is the only part of the ride that is steep. Turn right at the dam to go around the lake in a counterclockwise direction. After you pass the dam the road is relatively flat and easy and very scenic, set in dense forest, meandering around the lake. There are three wooden bridges that you can either walk your bike across or, for a little adventure, ride through the creek!

Lake Lagunitas

Photo: Phyllis Neumann

The road ends at some stone steps in front of the ranger's residence. Walk your bike down them before your final coast down the stairs to the trail that leads to the parking lot. The parking area has water, restrooms and picnic tables and lots of trails to explore.

Alternate Ride 7a: Lake Lagunitas to Bon Tempe Meadow (Easy—6 miles). From Lake Lagunitas take Sky Oaks Road (the paved road you drove in on) to a dirt road on your left called Bon Tempe Dam Trail. This road will take you to the dam separating Bon Tempe from Alpine Lake. At the bottom of the hill take the right fork and pick up Bullfrog Trail. Pedal up the gentle hill to Bon Tempe Meadow. Turn right onto Sky Oaks Road which will return you to Lake Lagunitas.

Alternate Ride 7b: Phoenix Lake to Lake Lagunitas (Easy—2½ miles). This is the most popular lake in the Water District — and the most crowded. Begin at Natalie Coffin Green Park in Ross, which can get so crowded with hikers and bicyclists on weekends that parking can be a real problem. Shaver Grade is a flat, heavily used fire road in a lovely forest setting. It has a mild grade up to Five Corners, where another, slightly steeper road will take you up to Lake Lagunitas.

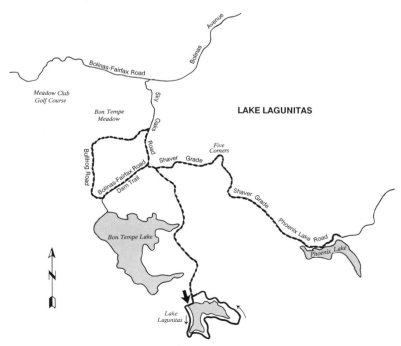

8. SAN RAFAEL
San Pedro Peninsula

Region: *Central Marin* **Rating:** *Medium*
Mileage: *14 Miles* **Riding Time:***1-2 Hours*
Type of Bike: *Touring or Mountain Bike*

Terrain: *Wide paved road with several moderate grades.*

Description: *A scenic tour around the San Pedro Peninsula on an excellent paved road with few cars. A good ride to take on a hot summer's day when you can enjoy swimming at McNear's Beach, about the halfway mark.*

Starting Location/Parking: *Start at the Marin Civic Center in San Rafael. From Highway 101, take the San Pedro Road exit onto San Pedro Road East. Turn left at Civic Center Drive and park your car next to the lagoon.*

Route: *Take Civic Center Drive to East San Pedro Road. Turn left at the light. Follow San Pedro Road around the Pensinula and into San Rafael where it becomes Third Street. Turn right onto Lincoln Avenue and over the bike path. Turn left on Los Ranchitos Road and right on North San Pedro Road to Civic Center Drive.*

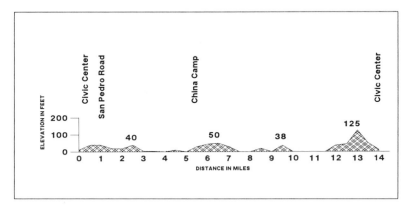

Begin your ride by turning left onto Civic Center Drive. At the light turn left on North San Pedro Road, a pleasant winding road through flat tidelands and small marshes. On the way out of town there is a designated bike path; however, on weekends cars line the path for several blocks.

Follow the road through the residential section of Santa Venetia. As you leave town the road feels more like country. A sign indicates winding road for the next 4 miles as it begins to climb into the country.

The open expanse of salt marsh leads to San Pablo Bay, and at several points San Pedro Road dips almost to sea level. San Francisco Bay used to have thousands of acres that resembled this area but most have been either filled in or dredged out over the years. There is no bike path to speak of, but very few cars use this road.

You will pass a sign that says: "China Camp State Park," and a few feet ahead will be Back Ranch Meadows Walk-in Campground. Cars left by campers line the road leading to the campground.

The road bends and curves as it follows the Bay. There are several vista points where you can view San Pablo Bay and take a break. Around one of the bends in the road is Buckeye Point, a picnic area on a little knoll.

The Bay stretches for miles and you can see on the far side the city of Point Richmond on the other side. Bullhead Flat is another vista point to the north. You can see the hangars of Hamilton Air Force Base and a glimpse of the Sonoma mountains.

China Camp Village   Photo: Cindy Neumann

China Camp Village was an old Chinese fishing village named *Wa Jen Ha Lio*, and was one of the earliest, largest, most productive and last surviving Chinese shrimp fishing villages in California. By 1870 the Chinese immigrants and their descendants introduced the use of commercial netting to catch bay shrimp off Point San Pedro. The shrimp were then dried and exported to China and throughout the world. The Visitor Center has a lovely exhibit of the history of China Camp. In the village there is a drinking fountain, pit toilets and a small cafe that sells drinks, sandwiches and even cooked shrimp. There are also miles of dirt fire roads for mountain bike exploration.

A few miles past the Village is *McNear's Beach Park,* a lovely county park with over 70 acres of lawn, swmming and wading pools, tennis courts, picnic tables, beach, restrooms and drinking water and great views. A recent addition has been the newly built cement fishing pier. Day use fee is $1.00 per person.

As you approach San Rafael a wide bike lane appears. Attractive homes line the road that overlook San Pablo Bay and the Richmond Bay Bridge. Two small islands, The Sisters, are visible in front of the bridge. On one of these the Lacatuit Indian, Chief Marin, sought refuge from the Spanish. When he was captured he was baptized at San Rafael. His name was later given to the county.

San Pedro Road becomes Third Street as it approaches Highway 101. Ride under the freeway and turn right onto Lincoln Avenue. Ride up the short hill at Fair Drive to the bike path by the fence that parallels the freeway. At the end of the fence turn left onto Los Ranchito Road. Much caution is needed here as this is a blind corner. Turn right on North San Pedro Road which takes you under the freeway. At the light turn left onto Civic Center Drive. This will bring you back to your car.

Alternate Ride 8a: Civic Center Lagoon (Easy—1 mile). Take a tour around the Civic Center and the Lake. It's a nice area. A paved path lets you tour the grounds around the Lagoon and Exhibit Hall. Try to plan your trip to coordinate with some of the activities and events scheduled at the Exhibit Hall.

The Farmers Market is held twice a week and is where the farmers of Marin and neighboring counties come to sell their produce directly to consumers. It is held in the parking lot of the Marin Civic Center Auditorium. Hours are: Thursdays, 8 a.m. to 1 p.m.; Sundays, 9 a.m. to 2 p.m. Admission is free.

The Marin County Civic Center is one of the most remarkable structures in Marin County and is visible from the freeway. This graceful building was designed by Frank Lloyd Wright and was his last major project before his death in 1959. The Civic Center is open from 8 a.m. to 5 p.m. Monday through Friday and is closed on legal holidays. Tours are available between 10 a.m. and 3:30 p.m. daily. There is no charge, and tours last about an hour; however, you must make arrangements at least three days in advance. Phone (415) 499-6396.

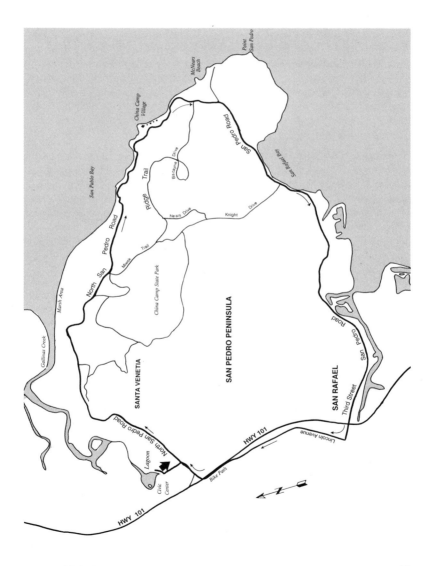

9. MT. TAMALPAIS STATE PARK
Ridgecrest Boulevard

Region: *Central Marin*   **Ratng:** *Medium*
Mileage: *8 miles*   **Riding Time:** *1½ hours*
Type of Bike: *Mountain or Touring Bike*

Terrain: *Paved road, rolling hills with fairly easy grades, no traffic.*

Description of Ride: *This ribbon of road, winding around the west side of Mt. Tamalpais, is one of the most photographed pieces of pavement in the world. Despite the constant filming, cyclists may still catch Ridgecrest on a quiet day, sharing it only with circling birds of prey, aloft on the ocean breezes. Here you will find dramatic, exceptional vistas of the Pacific coastline.*

Starting Location/Parking: *From Hwy 101 take the Stinson Beach exit. Follow signs to Mt. Tamalpais. Drive to the Rock Springs Parking Area on Panoramic Highway. If you are in good shape, you may start your ride at the Pantoll Ranger Station and ride up the steep road to the parking area by bike. Otherwise drive your car and start at the Rock Springs Parking Area.*

Route: *From the parking lot take Ridgecrest Blvd. north along the Bolinas Ridge. The paved road ends at the beginning of the Bolinas Ridge Trail. Return on the same road.*

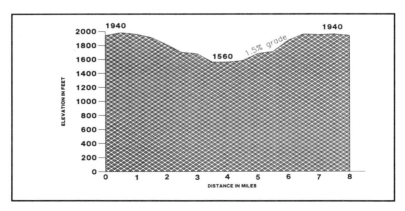

Mount Tamalpais State Park is one of the oldest and most popular parks in California, with over 6,300 acres, including Muir Woods National Monument. With an elevation of 2,571 feet Mt. Tam is the third highest mountain in the Bay Area, and among the most spectacular. Mount Tamalpais had become a popular tourist attraction by 1849 and the "Mill Valley and Mount Tamalpais Scenic Railway" was built to take tourists from Mill Valley to the summit. This 8-mile trip was often called the "Crookedest Railroad in the World" because of the 281 curves it took to get up the mountain. Most of the railroad line was destroyed by fire in 1929.

Mt. Tam (as is popularly called) has long been a favorite spot for hikers and equestrians, and, with the recent popularity of the mountain bike, is now being enjoyed for its biking trails. Bicycles are permitted only on paved and developed fire roads, and prohibited on hiking trails or paths. You may not ride, or even carry, your bicycle off the designated road or you may get a ticket. Maximum speed is 15 mph, unless posted. At blind turns, and when passing hikers and equestrians, 5 mph is required.

Park your bike at the Rock Springs Parking Area. Take Ridgecrest Blvd. north along the Bolinas Ridge. There are dramatic, exceptional vistas in any direction. On a clear day you can see forever across the Pacific. If you look down you can see Stinson Beach and Shoreline Hwy. This is a popular area for hang gliders and kite flyers and the road is often used in television car commercials. It is fairly level and is subject to closure to cars, especially in high fire times, so traffic is light to none.

The road is gentle and easy and follows along the top of the ridge high overlooking the Pacific. Mile after beautiful mile the road dips in and out of forest and grassy expanse. There's not a sound to be heard and every bend in the road gives you another angle of the vista.

Ridgecrest Blvd. ends at a three-road junction. At this point you can return to the Rock Springs Parking Area the way you came. A gate leads to the Bolinas Ridge Trail, which is a popular fire road for mountain bikes that is very scenic. If you have a mountain bike you might consider taking the Bolinas Ridge Trail, ending at Olema 11 miles away. The road to the right is the Bolinas-Fairfax Road, which is a very steep and winding road down to Alpine Lake, ending in Fairfax (8 miles). This road is often littered with rocks, tree branches and patches of loose dirt. The road to the left is also very steep and curvy and leads down to Shoreline Highway and Bolinas. These roads are not recommended unless you are experienced and in very good condition. If you are on a touring bike you will need to invoke much caution to be safe. The climbs back are tough.

Alternate Ride 9a: Rock Springs to East Peak (Challenging — 6 miles).
For a more challenging ride from the Rock Springs Parking Area, take East Ridgecrest Blvd. and follow

signs to the summit. This road climbs steadily to West Peak (2,571-foot elevation). There is relatively little shade and it can get hot. At the Air Force Base ("ice cream cone" radar domes) there is a short, but very steep section. It's a nice stop at the top here to get a breather and take in the magnificent view. Continue on to the summit. There is a downhill section followed by an uphill climb to the end of the road. The last section of road is divided and very narrow with no shoulder. Your reward for the climb is an exceptional vista of the San Francisco skyline and surrounding Bay Area. There is a refreshment stand, restrooms and water here. From here you will have to hike to the summit on the .7-mile Verna Dunshee Trail. Bikes are not allowed on this trail. The return trip is, of course, pretty easy.

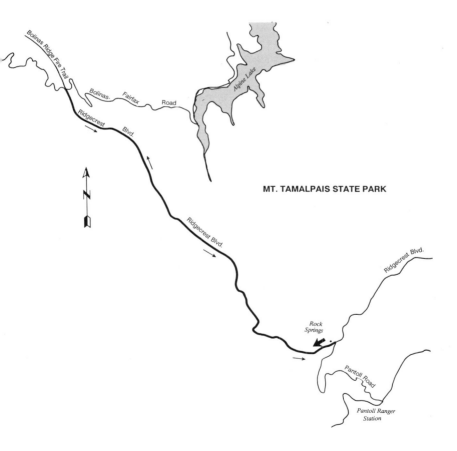

MT. TAMALPAIS STATE PARK

Central Marin

10. MT. TAMALPAIS STATE PARK
Old Stage Road

Region: *Mt. Tamalpais State Park*
Mileage: *8 miles*
Type of Bike: *Mountain Bike*

Rating: *Easy*
Riding Time: *1-1½ hours*

Terrain: *Easy, mild fire trail with short section of pavement.*

Starting Location/Parking: *Pantoll Ranger Station. From Hwy 101 take the Stinson Beach exit. Follow signs to Mt. Tamalpais, Stinson Beach, Muir Woods. Take Panoramic Highway to the Pantoll Ranger Station.*

Route: *Take the Old Stage Road up to West Point Inn. Continue on Old Railroad Grade to East Peak. Return the same way.*

Description of Ride: *This is a beautiful and gentle ride up to East Peak, and one of the most popular in the park. The road is a gradual uphill grade with several rest areas and spectacular views of the entire Bay Area. This is an excellent ride for beginners.*

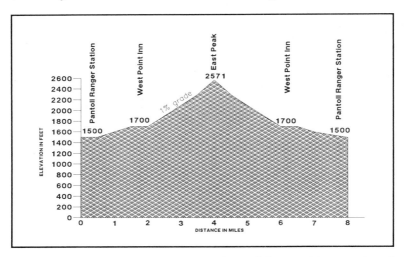

Begin at the Pantoll Ranger Station. Pick up Old Stage Road across the road from the parking lot. The trail begins very easily and starts to climb almost immediately. It is paved at this point. Follow the road up to West Point Inn (2 miles).

West Point Inn is a beautiful old lodge that is the traditional rest stop for hikers and bicyclists headed to the top of Mt. Tam. It was originally the farthest point that the railroad traveled on its way up to the summit. Today the Inn is owned by the Marin Municipal Water District where you can get water, restrooms and refreshments, and even stay overnight by reservation. This is a great place to take a break and view the magnificance around you.

From West Point Inn you will take Old Railroad Grade the remaining 1½-miles to up the summit. Since you will be sharing the road with hikers and equestrians, please be careful, especially around any blind turns.

At the end of Railroad Grade turn right onto East Ridgecrest Blvd. for the last section of paved road. The view from the summit is spectacular. You can see magnificent views of San Francisco and the Golden Gate Bridge. A graphic plate identifies scenic points of the entire Bay Area. There is a visitor center there, a refreshment stand, picnic tables, and restrooms. To get to the summit you must leave your bike behind and travel by foot. The .7-mile Verna Dunshee Trail will take you up to the top of East Peak where you can get a 360 degree view of Marin County and the Bay Area. The Gardiner Lookout is not open to the public. Return to the Pantoll Ranger Station on the same route.

East Peak on Mt. Tamalpais

Photo: Jeff Dooley

Alternate Ride 10a. Old Stage Road to West Point Inn (Easy — 4 miles). For an easy ride that's not very long or strenuous take Old Stage Road to West Point and return. There are spectacular views and refreshments and restrooms available.

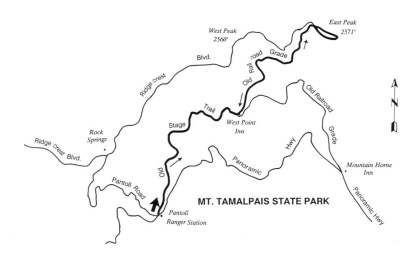

11. MT. TAMALPAIS STATE PARK
Old Railroad Grade

Region: *Central Marin*
Mileage: *11 miles*
Type of Bike: *Mountain Bike*

Rating: *Medium*
Riding Time: *2-3 Hours*
Max. Elevation: *2571 feet*

Terrain: *A mixture of paved roads and dirt fire trails that can be quite steep in places.*

Description of Ride: *One of the most popular rides for mountain bikes in Mt. Tamalpais. This road can get quite crowded, especially on weekends.*

Starting Location/Parking: *Start from the Mountain Home Inn Parking Lot on Panoramic Highway in Mill Valley. From Hwy 101 take the Stinson Beach exit and follow signs to Mt. Tamalpais.*

Route: *From the Parking Lot travel west on Panoramic Highway to the Pantoll Ranger Station. Take Pantoll Road to East Ridgecrest Blvd. Turn right and follow it to East Peak. From the summit pick up Old Railroad Grade where the two roads intersect. Follow it down to West Point Inn. Continue on Old Railroad Grade back down to Mountain Home Inn.*

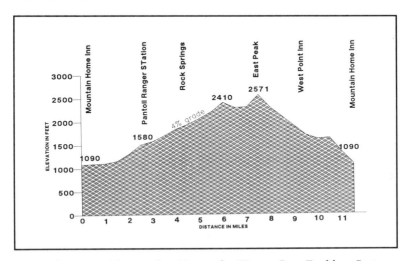

Begin your ride at the Mountain Home Inn Parking Lot on Panoramic Highway. From the parking lot take Panoramic Highway to the Pantoll Ranger Station (2½ miles). This is a steep paved road that can get a lot of traffic, especially on weekends. Restrooms and water are available at Pantoll.

Take Pantoll Road to East Ridgecrest Blvd. Ridgecrest Blvd. provides some spectacular views of the coastline and the Farallon Islands. This ride should be done early in the day otherwise traffic on Panoramic Highway becomes a problem.

The summit parking lot is often windy, cold and/or foggy. You may find relief from the cold at the Snack Wagon there. Restrooms, water and picnic tables are available. The view from the summit is spectacular. You can see magnificent views of San Francisco and the Golden Gate Bridge. A graphic plate identifies scenic points of the entire Bay Area.

Pick up Old Railroad Grade right where the two one-way roads from the parking lot intersect and take the trail down. The Grade is a steep, downhill dirt and gravel two-lane fire road that is well maintained. It is a series of "S" turns. You can take a breather at West Point Inn. Continue left on Old Railroad Grade until it intersects with Panoramic Highway at Mountain Home Inn Parking Lot, bringing you back to your starting point.

Alternate Ride 11a. Mountain Home Inn to West Point Inn (Easy—2 miles). A smooth easy climb that goes up the mountain

Old Railroad Grade   Photo: Jeff Dooley

with a break at West Point Inn. Return on the same route, or continue on to Pantoll Ranger Station and take Panoramic Highway back (8.7 miles).

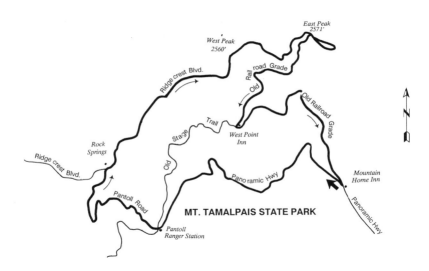

WEST MARIN

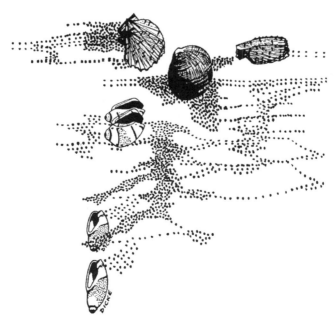

Stinson Beach

12. STINSON BEACH TO MUIR WOODS

Region: *West Marin*　　　　　　**Rating:** *Challenging*
Mileage: *20½ miles*　　　　　　**Riding Time:** *3-4 hours*
Type of Bike: *Mountain or Touring Bike*

Terrain: *Paved, smooth highway with some fairly steep climbs and moderate weekend traffic.*

Description: *Ride along the crest of beautiful Shoreline Highway with some of the most magnificent views of the Pacific coast anywhere. The ride leads you to a serene walk through Muir Woods — a ride you won't soon forget.*

Starting Location/Parking: *Begin at Stinson Beach State Park. From Hwy 101 take Stinson Beach exit and follow Shoreline Highway. At the junction where the road turns to Mt Tam and Muir Woods take the road on the left to Stinson Beach. Follow signs to Stinson Beach State Park.*

Route: *Begin your ride at Stinson Beach State Park. From the parking lot take Shoreline Highway north to Muir Woods Road and follow it 2 miles to Muir Woods. Return to Stinson Beach on the same route.*

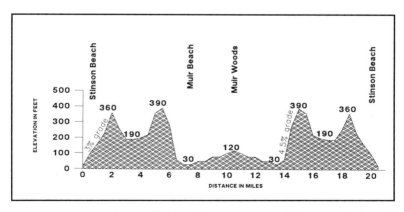

Stinson Beach is a quiet beach community with a population of about 400 and few commercial businesses. Go into town and, at the sign, turn left to Stinson Beach Park, where your ride begins.

Stinson Beach State Park, which includes some 53 acres, is open for picnicking, hiking, surfing, and fishing. Swimming is permitted from late May to mid-September, when lifeguards are on duty. There is a snack bar and picnic area. There is no day use fee.

From the parking lot follow the exit signs back to Shoreline Highway. Watch for cars pulling out in front of you or car doors suddenly opening. Cross the bridge at Eascoot Creek and continue through town. The road begins to climb almost immediately, giving you a sense of what's to come. Watch for traffic on the weekends; there is no bike path.

Stay on Shoreline Hwy as it climbs and winds around the headlands. Below you the Pacific coastline stretches majestically for miles in either direction. There are plenty of vista turnouts for stopping to look, and trails where you can walk down to the beach, should you so desire. If you look north you can see the town of Stinson Beach. If you look to the south on a clear day you can even see San Francisco.

The road continues to climb and wind around the cliffs. You can see the road leading down to the *Steep Ravine Environmental Campground* which is owned by Mount Tamalpais State Park and features ten rustic cabins and six primitive campsites.

View of Stinson Beach from Shoreline Highway   Photo: Phyllis Neumann

As the road begins to turn inland slightly you can view Mt. Tamalpais and the internal coastal valleys. You can also see Shoreline Highway down below as it passes through Muir Beach. It is now a downhill coast until you reach Muir Beach. Homes begin to dot the roadway and street signs become evident. Watch your speed!

At the junction you can decide to turn right and explore Muir Beach (½-mile), which is a nice place to stop for lunch, or turn left onto Muir Woods Road.

Muir Beach is a lovely semi-circular beach cove ½-mile from the junction on Shoreline Highway. Turn right on Pacific Way at Pelican Inn, a favorite restaurant and lodge. Continue up the road and over the bridge and through the woods to the Day Use Area parking. There are restrooms and picnic tables. From Muir Beach return to Shoreline Highway and turn left. At the junction you can bear left back to Stinson Beach or you can go continue on Muir Woods Road to Muir Woods.

Muir Woods Road is a wide, smoothly paved road with no bike path, and very little traffic, even on weekends. Follow the road 2½ miles to Muir Woods. This is a beautiful bike trail, surrounded by low coastal trees. Once you cross the bridge over the creek you enter Muir Woods National Monument. On weekends, because of the difficulty finding a parking space, cars are parked along the edge of the road leading to the parking area.

Muir Woods National Monument, part of Mt. Tamalpais State Park, contains one of the Bay Area's last uncut stands of old-growth redwoods (Sequoia sempervirens). Because the 295 acres of forest along Redwood Creek was hard to get to, it was spared from logging and purchased by Elizabeth Thacher Kent, who then donated the land to the Federal Government. In 1908, President Theodore Roosevelt declared it a national monument, with Kent naming it after conservationist, John Muir. The park has beautiful hiking trails through the dense growth of coastal redwoods. Lock your bike here and take a refreshing walk in the woods. Restrooms and water are available. The park is open daily from 8 a.m. to sunset.

Return to Stinson Beach by the same route.

Variation: Pantoll Ranger Station (Challenging — 17 miles). This route, with its 1300-foot climb, is not recommended for novice riders or children. Leave Muir Woods and continue up the very steep, narrow winding road, which can have heavy tourist traffic on weekends. There are magnificent views of coastal mountains and deep valleys. At the four corners intersection turn left onto Panoramic Highway. Continue about four miles up the side of Mt.

Tamalpais to the Pantoll Ranger Station. Water is available there. For your return to Stinson Beach continue downhill on Panoramic Highway down to Shoreline Highway. At the junction turn right to return to Stinson Beach.

Alternate Ride 12a: Muir Beach to Muir Woods (Easy—5 miles). This is a beautiful bike trail with a mild grade to Muir Woods. Begin at the Muir Beach Day Use parking area. From Muir Beach right on Pelican Way and left onto Shoreline Highway. Continue up Muir Woods Road to Muir Woods (2½ miles). The road is surrounded by low coastal trees and is wide and smoothly paved road with no bike path, and very little traffic, even on weekends. Return to Muir Beach on the same route.

Alternate Ride 12b. Stinson Beach to Bolinas (Easy—7 miles). A beautiful, easy ride around the Bolinas Lagoon. Because of the traffic on Shoreline Highway this ride is not recommended for children. Begin your ride at Stinson Beach and follow Shoreline Highway to the town of Bolinas, which is not marked and relatively difficult to find because people keep stealing the sign. Turn left on on Olema-Bolinas Road and left on Horsehoe Hill Road to town. Return to Stinson Beach on the same route.

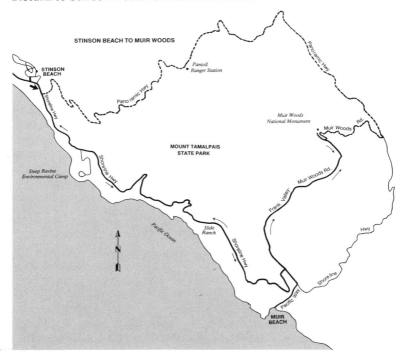

13. PT. REYES NATIONAL SEASHORE
Bear Valley Trail

Region: *West Marin*
Mileage: *9 miles*
Type of Bike: *Mountain Bike*

Rating: *Easy*
Riding Time: *1 hour*

Terrain: *A flat, wide forest trail that can get congested with hikers on weekends. No motorized vehicles are permitted.*

Description: *This very pretty trail takes you through a dense forest that follows a creek. It is the most popular one in the park and is exceptionally crowded with hikers on the weekends. Because of the congestion, it is recommended that cyclists use this trail only on weekdays. This is a very nice ride for the whole family.*

Starting Location/Parking: *Start at Pt. Reyes Park Headquarters outside of Olema. From Hwy 101 take the Sir Francis Drake exit and follow it to Olema. Turn left at the National Seashore to the Visitor Center*

Route: *From the parking lot at the Visitors' Center take Bear Valley Trail and follow it to the almost to the coast. Return on the same trail.*

Pt. Reyes National Seashore has over 150 miles of hiking, biking and equestrian trails. From Park Headquarters there are several trails for mountain bikes that go and return on the same trail, but there are no loop trips. There are four campgrounds within the park that are accessible by bike, but there are no biking trails near the campground that can be used for exploring the area. Advance reservations are advisable, as campsites fill quickly. Call 663-1092.

The Pt. Reyes Visitor Center has exhibits, an interesting film of Pt. Peyes history, Indian artifacts and a seismograph which monitors earthquake activity throught the world. Bikes are permitted on designated trails only. Do not ride, or even carry, your bike on trails other than designated bike trails or rangers may give you a ticket. Maps detailing these trails can be picked up at the Visitors' Center.

Bear Valley Trail is easy and follows lovely Bear Valley Creek. At Divide Meadow, 1½ miles from the entrance, there is an open grassland and a nice place for a stop. Pit toilets and picnic benches are set up nearby. The meadow got its name because the flow from the creek changes at this point, emptying out in the Pacific instead of Tomales Bay.

The trail ends for bicyclists at the Glen Trail junction, another meadow where the Park Service has placed a bicycle rack for those wishing to walk the .8 miles to Arch Rock and view the magnificent Pacific coastline. Return to the Visitor Center on the same road.

Visitor Center

OLEMA

Morgan Horse Ranch

Bear Valley Road

N

Bear

Valley

Trail

Divide Meadow

BEAR VALLEY TRAIL

Pacific Ocean

Arch Rock

Bear Valley Trail

Photo: Rawls Frazier

14. PT. REYES PENINSULA
Pt. Reyes Lighthouse

Region: *West Marin*　　　　**Rating:** *Challenging*
Mileage: *44½ miles*　　　　**Riding Time:** *5-6 hours*
Type of Bike: *Mountain or Touring Bike*

Terrain: *Smoothly paved road with little traffic with several impressive grades.*

Description: *A lovely scenic tour of the Pt. Reyes Peninsula, ending at the historic Pt. Reyes Lighthouse. The ride is a fairly challenging uphill ride with two significant grades. It should be taken in the morning because of the winds that come up in the afternoon.*

Starting Location/Parking: *Bear Valley Park Headquarters in Olema. From Hwy 101 take Sir Francis Drake Blvd. to Olema (about 26 miles). Turn left at Bear Valley Road 1 mile to the Visitors Center.*

Route: *From the Bear Valley Visitor Center turn left onto Bear Valley Road. Go 1½-miles to the stop sign and bear left onto Sir Francis Drake Highway (toward Inverness and beaches). Continue on Sir Francis Drake through Inverness, and follow signs to the Lighthouse. Return the same way.*

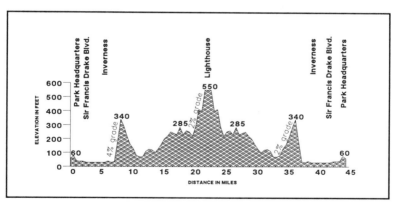

Begin your ride at Bear Valley Visitor Center. Park your car here. From the parking lot return to Bear Valley Road and turn left. Follow the sign to the Lighthouse and Beaches (15 miles). The road is smoothly paved and easy for this stretch of the ride. Oak trees line the road and there are few cars that pass, especially during weekdays.

At the stop sign at Sir Francis Drake Blvd. continue straight ahead. You will be paralleling Tomales Bay on your right. After 4½ miles you will pass through Inverness, which was named after Inverness, Scotland by Judge James McMillan Shafter because it reminded him of his heritage. Many street names and houses also reflect the Scottish tradition.

Right outside of Inverness there is a significant climb. At the junction bear left and continue on Sir Francis Drake Hwy. The road is relatively wide and smooth. You will pass through several cattle ranches with cattle grates that cannot be avoided. The scenery changes as you ride from forested road to open rolling hills with spectacular views. After several miles you will be able to see the Pacific Ocean on your right.

The ride ends at the Pt. Reyes Lighthouse and Lookout, which is about ¼-mile from the parking lot up a paved road. There is water at the lighthouse and a small Visitor Center. This is an excellent vantage point for whale watching. Facing east, you can also see the spectacular 10-mile narrow stretch of beach. Because of the pounding surf and strong undertow, swimming is prohibited, but there are great picnic spots as well as sand dunes and driftwood to investigate.

Pt. Reyes Lighthouse

Photo: Phyllis Neumann

On a clear day the Lookout is usually filled with whale watchers, hoping to catch a glimpse of the 15,000-20,000 whales passing by the Lighthouse each winter on their way to Baja, and returning to the Arctic waters each summer.

The Pt. Reyes Lighthouse, which was originally built in 1870 in France and shipped to the United States, is down a flight of 300 stairs. In 1975 an automated light was installed and the Lighthouse was retired. The Lighthouse is open every day from 10:00 a.m. to 5:00 p.m. except Tuesdays.

Alternate Ride 14a: Drakes Beach (Medium — 14 miles). Instead of riding all the way to the Lighthouse from the Pt. Reyes Visitor Center you might consider driving out to Drakes Beach. From there you can cycle up the hill and ride down to the Lighthouse (7 miles). Drakes Beach is a wide, flat beach that is sheltered from the wind. Because of the mild surf swimming is permitted. A snack bar is open in summer.

Alternate Ride 14b: Drakes Estero (Challenging — 9 miles). The beauty of the estero is worth the effort for this ride. You may have to walk your bike in several places because the roads are in poor condition. There are also several cattle gates that you may have carry your bike over.

Alternate Ride 14c: Limantour Beach (Challenging Ride–20 miles). From Park Headquarters turn left on Bear Valley Road and left on Limantour Road. The paved wide road has a wide bike path and with a steep grade up to 780-foot elevation. This is the most popular beach for swimming, picnicking, walking along the dunes and watching the extraordinary variety of birds.

Sir Francis Drake Highway   Photo: Phyllis Neumann

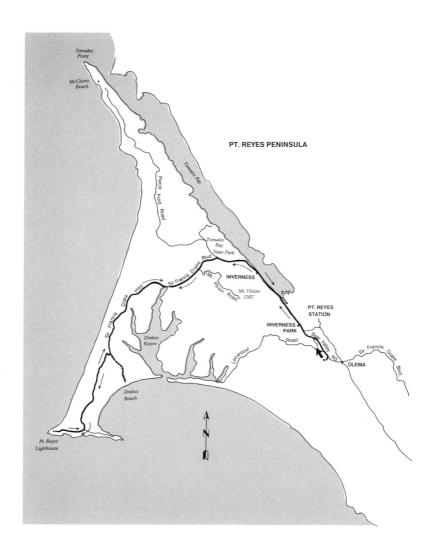

PT. REYES PENINSULA

15. PT. REYES PENINSULA
Mt. Vision Overlook

Region: *West Marin*   **Rating:** *Challenging*
Mileage: *15 miles*   **Riding Time:** *2½–3 hours*
Type of Bike: *Mountain Bike or Touring Bike*
Max. elevation: *1,336 feet*

Terrain: *Paved road with some substantial climbs, winding up the mountain. At the gate the road becomes a dirt fire road.*

Description: *This challenging ride has some incredibly beautiful views in a series of switchbacks climbing to 1,282 feet over 4 miles. There are breathtaking panoramic vistas of Pt. Reyes, the ocean, meadows and waterways that comprise Drakes' Estero. You can take a touring bike up the paved road to the summit and return to Pt. Reyes Station on the same route, but you will need a mountain bike if you intend to ride the fire trails past the gate.*

Starting Location/Parking: *Pt. Reyes Station. From Hwy 101 take Sir Francis Drake Blvd. to Olema (about 26 miles). Turn left at Bear Valley Road and go 1 mile to the Visitor Center.*

Route: *Take Shoreline Highway south from Pt. Reyes Station. Turn right on Sir Francis Drake Blvd. and follow it to the town of Inverness. At the junction (4 miles) bear left. The Mt. Vision left turnoff is a left turn off Sir Francis Drake Highway and is well marked.*

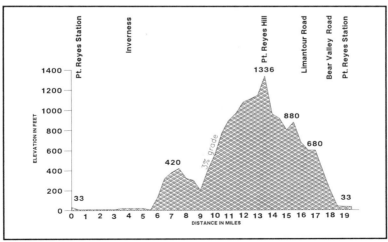

From Pt. Reyes Station follow Shoreline Highway south ¼-mile and turn right on Sir Francis Drake Blvd. After you pass through the town of Inverness (4 miles) there is a substantial climb. At the junction bear left toward the ocean. The Mt. Vision left turnoff is the first left turn off the Sir Francis Drake Highway after the junction. You immediataely begin to climb in a series of switchbacks, each bend in the road revealing more of the spectacular panorama.

At the vista point (1,282 feet) there is a turnout with a historical marker that identifies scenic points: Pt. Reyes, Chimney Rock and the Farallon Islands. If you do this ride early in the morning the sun will be behind you, shining out on the estero and ocean. Bring your camera. It is simply breathtaking!

A bit further up on your left there is a turnout that gives a spectacular view of Tomales Bay — another great camera shot. The paved road continues on, past the gate, to the summit of Pt. Reyes Hill (1,336 feet). At the top the views are spectacular and, on a clear day you can even see the Farallon Islands, 28 miles out at sea.

For those with mountain bikes, at pavement's end pick up the Inverness Ridge Trail (the Bucklin Trail starts here as well but is banned to bicycles). Inverness Ridge Trail starts out as a narrow (one-person wide) set of steep downhill switchbacks. After a few hundred yards it widens out to clay, shale trail and, after about one

View from Mt. Vision of Tomales Bay   Photo: Phyllis Neumann

drop in elevation. This is a challenging ride through a pine forest. The trail crests at a ridge and becomes a two-lane road. Here there is a long downhill coast. After about 3 miles of ups and downs the trail intersects with Limantour Road, a paved spectacular downhill of "S"-turns which ends near the Bear Valley Ranger Station. Take a break here, get a drink, then follow Shoreline Highway two miles back to Pt. Reyes Station.

Alternate Ride 15a: Pt. Reyes Station to Mt. Vision and Back (Challenging — 26 miles). This ride is for cyclists on touring bikes who would love to take in the beauty of Mt. Vision. Follow the road as described above to the top of Mt. Vision. Return on the same route.

Alternate Ride 15b: Pt. Reyes Station to Inverness (Easy — 9 miles). Consider riding only to the town of Inverness and back. The road is flat and scenic as it follows Tomales Bay.

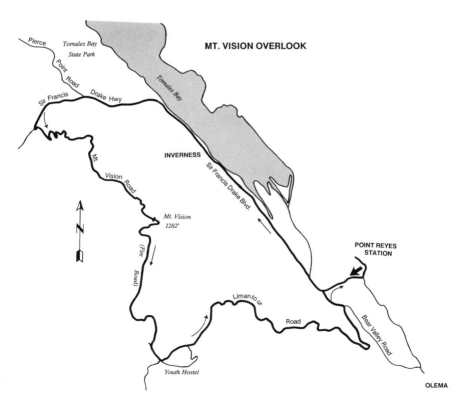

16. TOMALES BAY STATE PARK
Heart's Desire Beach

Region: *West Marin*
Mileage*: 19 miles*
Type of Bike: *Mountain or Touring Bike*

Rating: *Medium*
Riding Time: *1-2 hours*

Terrain: *Smooth, level paved road with very little traffic. After the town of Inverness the road has some moderate hills.*

Description: *A fairly gentle ride paralleling the beautiful Tomales Bay. The ride is level until Inverness and has some moderate climbs after that. A nice place to picnic at a lovely beach cove on Tomales Bay.*

Starting Location/Parking: *Pt. Reyes Station. From Hwy 101 take the Petaluma exit and turn on "D" Street to Pt. Reyes or exit Sir Francis Drake Hwy..*

Route: *From Pt. Reyes Station go south on Shoreline Highway 1/4-mile. Turn right and take Sir Francis Drake Blvd. past Inverness. At the junction bear right onto Pierce Point Road to the entrance to Tomales Bay State Park. Turn right into the park and follow it down the hill. At the bottom of the hill, turn left on the first road to Heart's Desire Beach. Return to Pt. Reyes on the same route.*

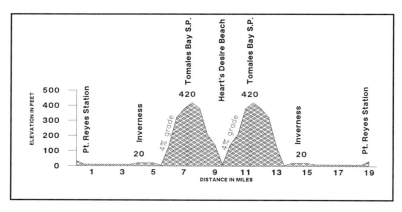

Tomales Bay State Park is a scenic recreation area located on the Point Reyes Peninsula. The three beaches — Indian, Heart's Desire, Pebble, and Shell beaches — are shallow and free of surf. The area was once a paradise for the Miwok Indians, and Indian mounds, or middens, are found along the beaches outside the park.

Begin in Pt. Reyes Station. Ride down Highway 1 over a short bridge and turn right onto Sir Francis Drake Blvd. Continue past the town of Inverness. At about 6½ miles go up a long steep hill. There's not much shoulder on this road. Just over the top of the hill bear right and turn onto Pierce Point Road toward Hearts Desire Beach (watch for the sign). At Tomales Bay State Park turn right and follow the road through a pretty pine forest until you reach the turnoff to Heart's Desire Beach, which is marked. This small beach cover is quite scenic and is a great spot for a picnic. There are restrooms and water available. Return to Pt. Reyes Station by the same route.

Alternate Ride 16a: Pierce Point Ranch (Challenging — 16 miles). The ride to Pierce Point Ranch is very scenic with rolling hills and panoramic views of Tomales Bay and the Pacific Ocean on each side of the peninsula. It's a lovely ride through pastureland, passing through several cattle ranches. The hills become steeper toward the end of the road with 500-foot grades. The land becomes more of a rugged, windswept plain, which is in sharp contrast to wooded area surrounding Inverness. Traffic is light. It can be quite windy in the afternoons. A high wooden fence marks the entrance to the Tule Elk Preserve a herd of over 80 elk. Pierce Point Ranch marks the end of the road, acting as a trailhead for paths leading to McClure's Beach and Tomales Point.

Heart's Desire Beach   Photo: Phyllis Neumann

Tomales Point, also known as Pierce Point, is where Tomales Bay and the Pacific Ocean meet. To reach this isolated beach you walk down a steep, twisted 4.5-mile trail; bicycles are prohibited. This beach can be cold and windy any time of year and is often shrouded in fog. Swimming is prohibited because of the riptides and undertow; however, this is a great place to explore the marine life in its natural habitat. Return to Pt. Reyes Station on the same route.

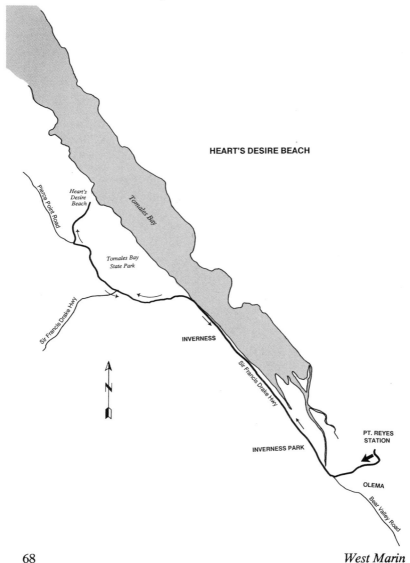

West Marin

17.THE BOLINAS RIDGE TRAIL

Region: *West Marin*
Mileage: *10 miles*
Type of Bike: *Mountain Bike*

Rating: *Medium*
Riding Time: *4 hours*
Max. Elevation: *1,719 feet*

Terrain: *A wide dirt fire road with rolling pastureland at the south end, passing through shady wooded sections toward the north.*

Description: *One of the most scenic and popular mountain bike trails in Marin County, the Bolinas Ridge Trail winds 11 miles from Olema to Fairfax-Bolinas Road, meandering over hills and through forests and cow pastures, offering expansive views of the Bolinas Lagoon, Inverness Ridge, Tomales Bay and Black Mountain   This ride only covers half of the actual trail*

Starting Location/Parking: *Samuel P. Taylor Park in Lagunitas on Sir Francis Drake Highway. From Hwy 101 take the Sir Francis Drake Blvd. Drive west through San Anselmo, Fairfax, Lagunitas and enter Samuel P. Taylor State Park. There is a $3.00 day use fee.*

Route: *From Samuel P. Taylor Park follow the paved bike path about 3 miles to the entrance gate of the Bolinas Ridge Trail. Continue along the ridge for about 5 miles to the Shafter Bridge Trail turnoff. In summer you can cross Lagunitas Creek and pick up the dirt fire road on the other side of Sir Francis Drake Highway. In winter, when the creek is full, you will have to take Sir Francis Drake Highway until it brings you back to the Park Entrance.*

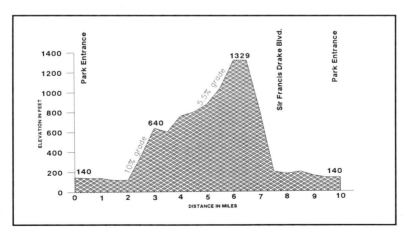

The Bolinas Trail is part of the Golden Gate National Recreation Area (GGNRA). It runs parallel to Shoreline Highway, rolling through pasturelands and stands of redwood. It is an ideal area for picnics, bird watching or just sunbathing. The trail is well traveled by hikers and horses, so be alert for them.

The Bolinas Ridge Trail can be reached from several trailheads along Sir Francis Drake Highway at the north end and from the Bolinas-Fairfax Road at the south end. Start in Samuel P. Taylor Park. Ride the paved bike trail through the park until you reach two wooden posts in the middle of the road. There is a metal sign designating "Bolinas Ridge." Go through the spring gate on your left and follow the dirt road up to the top of the ridge.

You can also reach the trail in Tocoloma, 3 miles north of the Park entrance. You will find parking off the side of the road, saving yourself the $3.00 day use fee. Take the paved bike path under the Sir Francis Drake bridge and follow the road to the entrance of the Bolinas Ridge Trail, as described above. The third entrance is at the top of Olema Hill where you can avoid the initial grade up to the ridge.

Once on the top of the Ridge you feel you are on top of the world with breathtaking views of the Olema Valley and Tomales Bay. If it is

Bolinas Ridge Trail

Photo: Jeff Dooley

spring the area is a rich green carpet sprinkled with wild flowers. The trail is full of rolling hills with open pastureland and grazing cattle. You will have to get off your bike to open the several cattle gates you encounter. After several miles the road takes you through a beautiful redwood grove. You will approach a junction where you can decide to leave the Ridge and return to the Park or continue on another 6 miles ending on Ridgecrest Blvd. in Mt. Tamalpais State Park.

If you decide to descend at this point take the Shafter Bridge turnoff down a steep but wide trail as it winds around the mountain with several switchbacks. You will end at Lagunitas Creek next to Sir Francis Drake Highway. If it is summer the Creek will be fairly low and you can ride your bike across without getting too wet. From here you can take the fire road across the highway. Turn left on this road to bring you back to the park entrance and your car. If it is winter then the Creek will be rather deep and it would be better to take Sir Francis Drake Highway back to the park entrance.

Alternate Ride 17a: Olema Hill to Shafter Bridge Turnoff (Medium — 10 miles).

An easier, more level ride begins at the top of Olema Hill, 1 mile east of Olema on Sir Francis Drake Blvd. Here you can avoid the initial grade up to the top of the Ridge. The trailhead starts at about 300 feet, heads south and follows the contour of the hill to the ridgeline. The trail gradually ascends for about 7 miles to 1,300 feet through open pastures. Be prepared to hoist your bike over gates. Take the trail to the Shafter Bridge turnoff and return on the same route. Or you can continue to the Bolinas-Fairfax Road for a spectacular ride back to Olema.

Alternate Ride 17b: Bolinas Ridge Trail to Olema (Challenging — 25 miles, dirt 11 miles).

This ride begins at the south end of the Bolinas Trail and heads north. Begin the ride at the top of Bolinas-Fairfax Road near the town of Bolinas and is well marked. The Bolinas-Fairfax Road is a series of switchbacks that climb to 1,400 feet over about 3½ miles from Shoreline Highway. The trail starts as a fire road on coarse gravel and clay bordered with scrub brush and pines. After the summit comes a steep downhill into and through an area of redwoods. Here you are actually east of the ridge and the trail is well marked. The trail returns to the ridge and travels through cow pastures. The last approximately 8 miles of this downhill run has 4-6 gates that separate cow pastures. All or none of them may be open. Be prepared to hoist your bike over fences. The trail ends at Olema on Sir Francis Drake Blvd. Return along Shoreline Highway to your car on the Bolinas-Fairfax Road.

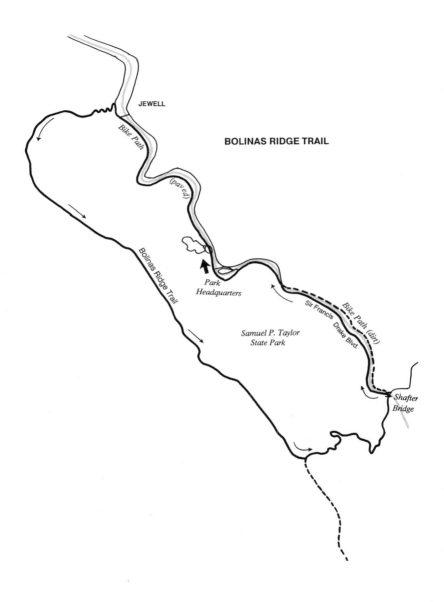

JEWELL

BOLINAS RIDGE TRAIL

Bike Path

(paved)

Bolinas Ridge Trail

Park
Headquarters

Samuel P. Taylor
State Park

Sir Francis
Drake Blvd

Bike Path (dirt)

Shafter
Bridge

NORTH MARIN

18. NICASIO RESERVOIR

Region: *North Marin*　　　　　　**Rating:** *Medium*
Mileage: *22 miles*　　　　　　　**Riding Time:** *2-3 hours*
Type of Bike: *Mountain or Touring Bike*

Terrain: *Wide paved road with bike paths on most roads. There is a moderate climb at the beginning of the ride, with the rest of the ride being fairly level with gently rolling hills.*

Description: *A beautiful, peaceful ride with little traffic on smooth country roads with moderate rolling hills. Be sure to take this ride clockwise to avoid strong winds that come up during the day.*

Starting Location/Parking: *Begin your ride in Nicasio, located on Nicasio Valley Road between Pt. Reyes-Petaluma Road and Lucas Valley Road. From Hwy 101 take the Lucas Valley Road exit.*

Route: *From the town of Nicasio take Nicasio Valley Road south out of town for 5 miles. Turn right on Sir Francis Drake Blvd. and follow it through Samuel P. Taylor State Park. Enter the park and take the paved bike trail to Platform Bridge Road. Connect with Pt. Reyes-Petaluma Road and go past the reservoir. Turn right on Nicasio Valley Road back to Nicasio and your car.*

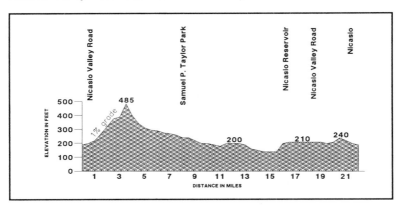

The town of Nicasio looks like it hasn't changed much since the turn of the century. Most buildings surround the small square with the ball playing field as its central attraction. The small church, Old St. Marys, was established in 1867.

Take Nicasio Valley Road south out of town. The road is peaceful and quiet with a small bike path. Though the bike path all but disappears there is very little traffic to worry about.

You will now be entering a more forested area with groves of redwood trees lining the road. The road starts climbing more heavily and, although you've been climbing from Nicasio, you begin to really feel it now. It levels out rather quickly as it is only a short hill. The shade brings relief on a warm day.

From the top of the hill you can look down to the valley below and see the San Geronimo Golf Course and Sir Francis Drake Blvd. a ½-mile descent brings you to the golf course you just saw at the top of the hill.

Turn right onto Sir Francis Drake Blvd. This road has some traffic but the road is smooth and fairly flat and has a wide bike lane. As soon as you enter a forested area the bike path disappears as the road also gets narrower and becomes more winding, moving in and out of forest.

You will be entering Samuel P. Taylor Park. There is a creek on the right below and is very scenic. There is no bike path to speak of but the road will accommodate you and the cars fairly well. If you look across the creek you can just make out the dirt fire road that is used by mountain bikes, joggers, and equestrians.

Nicasio Reservoir

Photo: Phyllis Neumann

Samuel P. Taylor Park has 2,600 acres of fern-filled groves of coast redwood trees. This area is best enjoyed during the spring and until early summer when temperatures are mild and the hills are still lush and green. After that they become dry and brown without rain. The park has a network of hiking trails and fire roads that are open for exploration. Overnight camping is available in the park and a special camping area has been reserved for bicyclists. For reservation information call MISTRIX at (800) 444-7275.

A paved 3-mile bike trail runs from the park entrance west to Tocaloma and is ideal for the whole family because it is nearly level, and quite scenic and motorized vehicles are prohbited.

At the brown "Bike Path" sign, turn right on Platform Bridge Road going toward Petaluma. You can take an alternate route to Olema and Pt. Reyes Station if you bear left on Sir Francis Drake Blvd. The road is free of traffic, through the hills. At the stop sign continue straight on toward Petaluma. The landscape changes dramatically from the lush forest to the more sparsely grown tress representing more of the coastal area.

After you pass the bridge on your left the road begins to climb rather steeply for quite a while. At the top of the hill is a fantastic overlook of the Nicasio Reservoir, which stores water for the San Geronimo Valley and East Marin. The area is almost devoid of trees and vegetation, looking more like desert terrain. Black Mountain can be seen to the west of the reservoir. Turn right at Nicasio Valley Road following the Reservoir around back to Nicasio and your car.

Variation #1. Pt. Reyes (Medium — 8-mile extension): For an extended scenic ride through the towns of Olema and Pt. Reyes continue straight on Sir Francis Drake Blvd. instead of turning on Platform Bridge Road. There is a fairly moderate climb just past Platform Bridge Road. *Olema* sits directly over the San Andreas Fault and was the epicenter of the 1906 earthquake that devasted San Francisco. The peninsula was thrust 16 feet northwestward at this point. At Shoreline Highway turn right and follow the road to Pt. Reyes Station, a lovely coastal town reminiscent of the old west. Ride through town and then turn right on Point Reyes-Petaluma Road. At the junction at Platform Bridge Road keep left and continue the ride as above.

Variation #2. The Cheese Factory (Challenging — 16-mile extension). Instead of turning right on Nicasio Valley Road continue on Point Reyes-Petaluma Road. There is a steep hill out of the reservoir. There is no shoulder and it can get hot in the summer. Continue until you reach the Cheese Factory where you can buy cheese, wine, and bread and have a lovely picnic by the duck pond. Return to Nicasio Valley Road, turn left and complete the ride as described above.

Alternate Ride 18a: Samuel P. Taylor Park Bike Path (Easy — 6 miles). Spend the day exploring the many bike trails in the Samuel P. Taylor Park and have a picnic lunch by Lagunitas Creek. There is a $3.00 day use fee. After entering the park ride along the paved road past the day use picnic area. Turn left across the bridge over Lagunitas Creek. Continue on the west side of the creek to the gate (there is an opening for bikes). Ride past the park service areas through another gate and onto a paved bike path. Follow this path to the end, where it crosses underneath Sir Francis Drake Blvd. and stops at Platform Bridge Road. Return the same way.

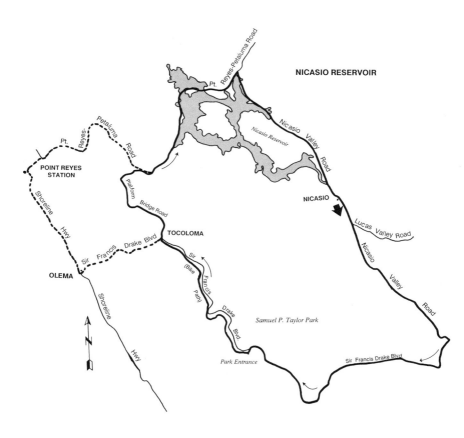

19. NOVATO
To The Cheese Factory

Region: *North Marin*
Mileage: *36 miles*
Type of Bike: *Mountain or Touring Bike*

Rating: *Challenging*
Riding Time: *4-5 hours*

Terrain: *Paved road with some moderate to steep hills.*

Description of Ride: *An exhilarating ride into the country with a picnic lunch at the Cheese Factory. Beautiful smoothly paved roads with little traffic. There are afternoon headwinds going out, but nice tailwinds on your return trip.*

Starting Location/Parking: *From Highway 101 take San Marin/Atherton Exit. Follow San Marin Drive to San Marin High School. San Marin Drive becomes Sutro Blvd. at the intersection. Park your car at the corner of Novato Blvd and Sutro Blvd.*

Route: *Go north on Novato Blvd. 6 miles. At the intersection of Petaluma-Pt. Reyes Road turn left (Cheese Factory sign). From the Cheese Factory continue for 3½ miles to Nicasio Valley Road. Take that to Lucas Valley Road. Go 10 miles and turn left at the first stoplilght on Las Gallinas Avenue. At Las Gallinas turn left. Pick up the bike path to Alameda del Prado, turn left on Ignacio Blvd., right on Sunset Parkway, left on Cambridge Street, left on Arthur Street, right on Indian Valley Road, left on Hill Road. Turn left at Center Road to Sutro Avenue. Right on Sutro to Novato Blvd. and your car.*

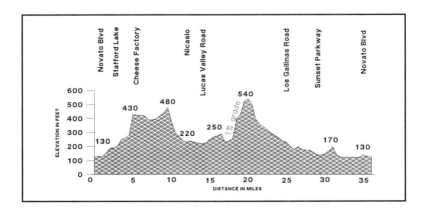

Begin your ride at the corner of San Marin Drive and Novato Blvd. Turn right on Novato Blvd and head north. A bike path is on the left side of the road and will help you avoid some of the traffic. The road heads out of the city limits and into the country. There are few cars but lots of joggers and bicyclists on the bike path. The bike path moves away from the road at a wooden fence and avoids the climb. It is relatively flat along here. The bike route parallels the road around, past the dam, and into Stafford Park. This is a lovely place for a breather.

From the park return to Novato Blvd. and continue on. The road has narrow shoulders and begins to climb. There is no bike path but traffic is light. The area is rolling pasture land with occasional houses. You feel you are in the country on a peaceful two-lane road. You will pass small herds of cattle grazing and old dairy barns.

The road continues to climb and wind around through the hills. It becomes fairly steep and peaks out. The road now becomes fairly level for a short while before it begins to climb again. At the intersection of Petaluma-Pt. Reyes Road turn left (there is a sign for the Cheese Factory here). The Cheese Factory is about ½-mile just over a small rise, past the Hicks Valley Fire Station.

The Marin French Cheese Company has been making French cheese since 1865. They produce four types of cheeses — Breakfast Cheese (mildest), Brie (delicate and creamy), Camembert (nutty,

Marin French Cheese Company

tangy flavor) and Schloss (strongest flavored). The process involves small round molds of cheese being turned and aged until ready to eat. Tours of the plant are offered 10 a.m. to 4 p.m. At the Cheese Factory you can decide to return on the same route or to continue on and take the loop trip. Whatever you decide to do The Cheese Factory is a great place for a picnic lunch.

When you leave the Cheese Factory turn right. The road levels out and continues to wind around the hills. The road has narrow shoulders, so be careful when riding on this road. The road begins some small climbs on rolling hills. There is a short hill then down a steep hill to the Nicasio Reservoir. The scenery is spectacular rolling pastureland with few trees and bushes. It resembles a desert scene in summer because it's so dry.

Just ahead you can see the Nicasio Reservoir. Turn left at Nicasio Valley Road, which crosses over the reservoir. Continue past the town of Nicasio. Turn left onto Lucas Valley Road, where you find yourself immediately in a redwood forest, which provides great shade on a warm day. There is no bike path, but there are few cars to worry about. The road is fairly level at the start and just beautiful. There is a climb up to the peak of the hill. At the top you can look down into the entire Lucas Valley. It is quite breathtaking. The narrow, corkscrew road carries you down into the valley floor rather rapidly. Watch your speed!

Suddenly the countryside gives way to a broader road with a bike path and civilization with a housing development. It seems you can't have one without the other. The road is quite level now with street signs and houses on your left and the creekbed on the right.

At Las Gallinas Avenue (stoplight) turn left. This brings you to the town of Marinwood. Continue on Las Gallinas to Miller Creek Road. Turn right toward Highway 101. At Marinwood Avenue pick up the bike path on the left side of the road. Follow it along Highway 101 to Alameda del Prado. Continue on paralleling the freeway until you reach Ignacio Blvd. Turn left. There is a smoothly paved road that goes through military housing and a wide bike path. The road is lined with trees. If you would like to tour Indian Valley College continue straight on Ignacio Blvd

Turn right on Sunset Parkway and up a short hill. Turn left on Cambridge Street. Turn left on Arthur Street (stop sign), right onto Indian Valley Road and bear left onto Hill Road. Follow Hill Road to the intersection with Tamalpais and turn right. Turn left at Center Road. Follow Center to Sutro Avenue and turn right. Returning you to San Marin High School.

Alternate Ride 19a: Stafford Lake (Easy—5 miles). Take the whole family for a picnic at Stafford Lake on this short, easy ride along a bike path. From Novato Blvd. head north out of town. Follow the path about 2½ miles to Stafford Lake. The route passes by a dam and enters the park at northeast end of the lake. Ride around the north end of the lake where there are picnic tables and barbecue pits. The area is very pretty. Return on the same bike route.

Alternate Ride 19b: Marin Cheese Factory and Back (Medium—13 miles). From Novato consider a shorter ride to the Cheese Factory. Avoid the major hills and picnic at the duck pond. Return to Novato by reversing your route.

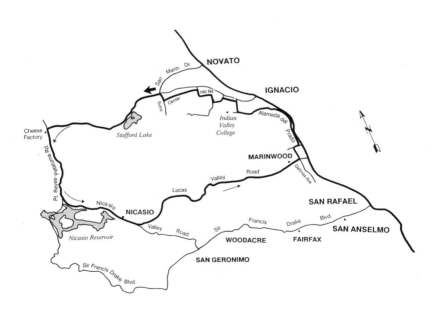

20. NOVATO
Mt. Burdell Open Space Preserve

Region: *North Marin*
Mileage: *6 miles*
Type of Bike: *Mountain Bike*

Rating: *Challenging*
Riding Time: *2 hours*
Max. Elevation: *1,450 feet*

Terrain: *Graded dirt fire road with sections of course gravel.*

Description: *This ride follows the path of the 10km Mt. Burdell Challenge Run. It takes you to the summit where you be rewarded with a panorama of San Pablo Bay.*

Starting Location/Parking: *From Highway 101 take San Marin/Atherton Drive. Follow San Marin Drive to San Andreas Drive. Turn right at the stop sign on San Andreas Drive past the Rolling Hills Country Club to the entrance to Mt. Burdell Open Space. Though the main gate is locked there is a green cattle gate (with a picture of a cow on it) which will give you access to the park.*

Route: *From the end of San Andreas Drive, follow the main fire road for about 1 mile, turn right at the first "Y" and take the uphill path at all the following junctions and you will reach the Sumit.*

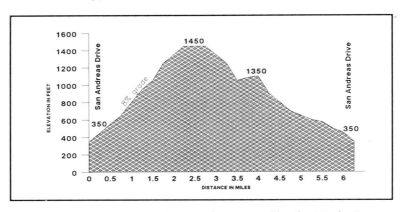

Mt. Burdell Open Space Preserve is managed by the Marin County Open Space District. This 1558-acre preserve adjoins 700 acres of the Rancho Olompali State Historic Park at the top of the mountain near its 1500-foot summit.

Mt. Burdell was originally inhabited by the local Miwok Indians, the Olompali people, and named for Mr. Galen Burdell. In the 1800s his wife, Marie Black, developed a farm famed for its walnut orchard, citrus groves, and vineyards on the lower slopes of the Rancho. The stone wall along the top of the mountain was built for them by Chinese laborers after the Gold Rush.

From March to May the slopes and meadows are green and covered with bright yellow buttercups, purple lupine and clusters of shooting stars. Bicycles are allowed on fire protection roads only, with a maximum speed of 15 mph, and 5 mph when passing others or rounding a blind turn.

From the end of San Andreas Drive, follow the main fire road for about 1 mile, turn right at the first "Y" and climb uphill, bearing right at all the following junctions, and you will reach the summit. After the first "Y" the switchbacks lead to Hidden Lake, which, through early May, is beautiful — a reflecting pool of water surrounded by a green carpet of grasses.

Take the left fork of the road following the steep uphill route toward the summit. At Big Oak junction continue upwards to the summit. Just below the summit is an AT&T tower and a paved maintenance road. From this road there are beautiful views to the west toward Pt. Reyes and, to the south, Novato and the Bay. Visible about 100 yards below the summit are stone walls built by Chinese laborers about 1875, defining the boundaries of Rancho Olompali as it once existed. A walk to the summit is rewarded by beautiful vistas of San Pablo Bay, Burdell Island and north toward Petaluma.

The ride down is an enjoyable coast! Retrace the uphill trail to Big Oak junction, then turn left (instead of right to Hidden Lake), follow the road to Deer Camp Spring and on to the San Andreas entry point. Allow at least 40 minutes for the uphill portion and 15-20 minutes for the return to San Andreas Drive.

Alternate Ride 20a: Hidden Lake (Medium — 5 miles). This is less steep than the Summit ride and is quite scenic. The first mile is moderately steep, but then the roads follows the contours for an easy ride. Enter the Mt. Burdell Open Space at San Carlos Way. Turn right on the fire road, go about 200 yards, turn left and follow it about 1 mile up the face of a ridge. When you see the cattle watering trough at the base of a large oak tree you are near the end of the steep section. This is a beautiful meadow area that is lush green between January and June. After the watering trough there is a plateau and "Y" in the road. Turn right (heading east) toward the old rock quarry. Stay on the road and turn left at the first green metal cattle gate (if you go through it, you exit the open space lands). Here you enter a wooded area. Follow the road through the second green gate and continue uphill at the next "Y" through the third green gate. Pause here to admire the view out over the Novato Valley. Follow the main road about 2 miles to Hidden Lake. Follow the main road down to the San Andreas Drive exit and follow it to San Marin Drive. Turn left to the San Carlos Way starting point.

21.

TOMALES
Whitaker Bluff Loop

Region: *North Marin* **Rating:** *Medium*
Mileage: *11 miles* **Riding Time:** *1-2 hours*
Type of Bike: *Mountain or Touring Bike*

Terrain: *Paved roads with gentle to steep rolling hills.*

Ride Description: *The roads around Tomales take you through the picturesque countryside of northern Marin County. They are two-lane paved country roads with little or no traffic that meander quietly along through rolling hills and dairies. There are several rides that can be taken using Tomales as a starting point. This ride is scenic and peaceful and has several steep grades. Most rides should probably be taken in the morning due to strong headwinds coming up in the afternoon.*

Starting Location/Parking: *Begin in the town of Tomales. From Hwy 101 take the East Washington Street exit in Petaluma and follow it out past the town of Two Rock. Bear left to Tomales.*

Route: *From Tomales take Shoreline Highway north out of town. Turn left onto Whitaker Bluff Road and left at Vallely Ford-Franklin School Road, which will take you back to Tomales.*

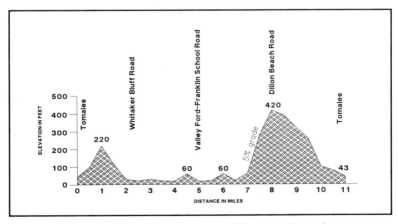

Tomales is a peaceful rural town. In the 1880s Tomales was once second to San Rafael in importance among Marin towns as a major dairy, shipping and rail center. Tomales also has the only high school in West Marin.

From Tomales take Shoreline Highway north out of town. This is a gentle road with Eucalyptus trees lining it. Turn left onto Whitaker Bluff Road. The road follows the Estero de Antonio on the left and begins a mild climb. Turn left at Valley Ford-Franklin School Road. The road begins to climb pretty quickly now. At the top of the hill is a magnificent view of the pasture lands dotted with stone outcroppings. You really get a sense of the countryside as you coast down the hill.

At Dillon Beach Road turn right and stop for a picnic lunch at Elephant Rocks. Here you can decide if you want to visit Dillon Beach or continue down the hill on this road. Dillon Beach is still run by the Lawson family, who came to the area in the 1920s. They offer a campground and marina. After leaving Elephant Rock continue on Valley Ford-Franklin School Road as it continues to turn inland, eventually taking you back to Tomales.

Alternate Ride 21a: Middle Road (Easy — 6½ miles). A similar ride but shorter and a bit easier. From the town of Tomales take Shoreline Hwy north out of town. The road begins to climb just a bit. Small old homes dot the highway. On your right sheep graze. The road is lined with eucalyptus trees. Turn left at Whitaker-Bluff Road and left again on Middle Road. Continue on past sheep

View of Tomales Bay from Elephant Rock   Photo: Phyllis Neumann

ranches and old dairy farms. At Dillon Beach Road turn left. This road is just magnificent as it winds along the hills. The road has little or no traffic but there is no bike path either. Stay to your right and be careful, especially on weekends.

Alternate Ride 21b: Marshall-Petaluma Road (Challenging — 36 miles). This ride climbs sharply in Marshall to 650 feet as it crosses the Bolinas Ridge with some spectacular views. Although it's a difficult grade it is well worth the views at the top that you can see in any direction. From Tomales take Shoreline Hwy south and follow Tomales Bay to Marshall and continue to Chileno Valley Road. Go 3 miles then turn left. It is still Cheleno Valley Road, but straight will carry you into Petaluma. At the Tomales-Petaluma Road turn left to return to Tomales. Turn left on Marshall-Petaluma Road.

Alternate Ride 21c: Tomales to Valley Ford (Challenging — 17 miles). This ride is very scenic but has some steep climbs. From Tomales take Dillon Beach Road 2½ miles, which becomes Valley Ford-Franklin School Road at the coast, 6 miles. This road will lead you right to Valley Ford. Turn right on Valley Ford Road, past Valley Ford to Middle Road (Slaughterhouse Road) 1 mile and turn right again. At Whitaker Bluff turn left and then a quick right to an unmarked road and take that to Dillon Beach Road. Turn left to Shoreline Highway back to Tomales.

Alternate Ride 21d: Fallon-Two Rock Road (Medium — 9½ miles). This ride is fairly easy, with gently rolling hills, taking you into the heart of Marin farmlands. From Tomales take Shoreline Highway north out of town 2½ miles. Climb the hill and turn right on Fallon-Two Rock Road. Cross Stemple Creek. The road travels through country farms and old ranches for another 2½ miles. Turn right on Twin Bridge Road. This road has gently rolling hillls with several grades. Turn right on Tomales-Petaluma Road, which will eventually return you to the town of Tomales.

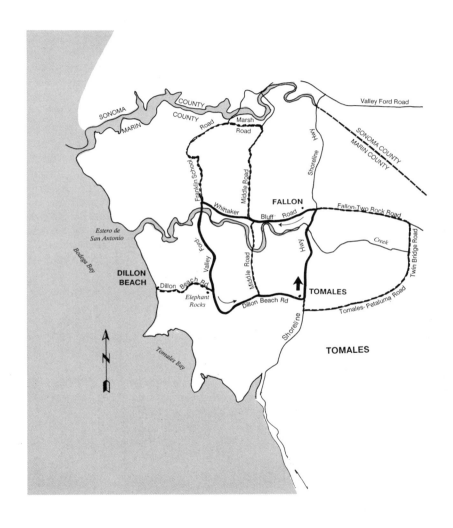

North Marin

HIGHWAY 101 ACCESS ROUTE

*The good building
is not one that hurts the landscape,
but one that makes the landscape
more beautiful than it was
before that building was built.*

— *Frank Lloyd Wright*

Marin County Civic Center

Highway 101 Access Route
Petaluma to the Golden Gate Bridge

Region: *North Marin*
Mileage: *44½ miles one way*
Type of Bike: *Touring or Mountain Bike*

Rating: *Challenging*
Riding Time: *5-6 hours*

Terrain: *Paved bike lanes, moderate to steep climbs, some freeway riding.*

DESCRIPTION: *This ride is included in the book as an access route for those needing to travel through Marin County as part of a tour or as a way of going from one city to another. It is not intended so much as a pleasure ride, but rather as a means to an end.*

Highway 101 becomes a divided highway in several places and there is no other access road, so, although it contains high-speed freeway traffic, it is sometimes necessary to use it. This route can get a bit tricky in spots, just locating some of the back roads, so study the map carefully.

STARTING LOCATION/PARKING: *The route described is from north to south. You can begin your trip from two locations: Petaluma or Novato.*

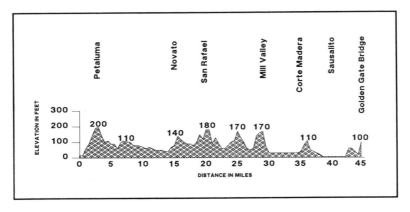

Petaluma to Novato

Begin your trip at Walnut Park on Petaluma Blvd. South. Continue down Petaluma Blvd. until you reach Highway 101 going south (bikes are allowed here). Travel on the wide shoulder (CAUTION! High-speed freeway traffic!)

As a longer alternative, but more scenic route through the back roads of Petaluma, start at Walnut Park and take 6th Street to "I" Street. Turn right on "I" Street south out of town. Continue to San Antonio Road and turn left. The road will come to a "T" with a small bridge on the right. Go over the bridge and continue to Highway 101.

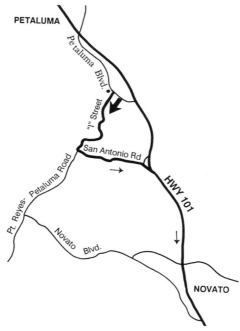

Petaluma to Novato

Novato to Ignacio

When you reach the outskirts of Novato look for the sign which says, "Bicycles Must Exit." This is at the McGraw-Hill building. Go through the opening in the fence to the frontage road.

Travel on the frontage road (Burdell Road) to the intersection of San Marin Drive and Redwood Blvd. (at the light). Continue straight on Redwood Blvd. for 2 miles to Rowland Blvd. Turn right on Rowland Blvd. Cross South Novato Blvd. and turn next left onto Cambridge Street (less than ½-mile) at the stop sign.

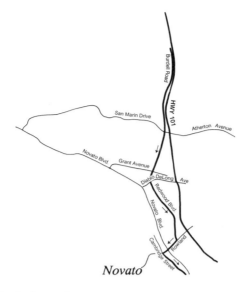

Novato

From Novato to Ignacio

From Cambridge Street turn right onto Sunset Parkway. Go over the hill and turn left onto Ignacio Blvd. (stop sign). (If you would like to see Indian Valley College turn right here.) Follow Ignacio Blvd. to Alameda Del Prado (1¾ miles) and turn right.

Continue to the bike path just past Burger King. The bike path entrance is on the east side of Alameda Del Prado, just right of the freeway entrance that "T"s into Alameda Del Prado.

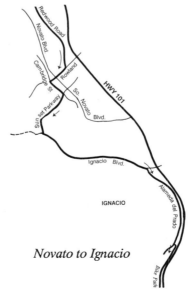

Novato to Ignacio

Marinwood to Terra Linda

Follow the bike path up and over to Miller Creek Road. Watch for bicycles coming in the opposite direction, especially on the downhill section. You will need to control your speed. CAUTION! At the end of the bike path is a metal pole dividing the lanes. The bike path emerges onto Miller Creek heading west, away from the freeway. Follow it to Las Galinas Avenue (at the stop sign).

Turn left onto Las Galinas. Take this to the Northgate Shopping Center. You will cross Lucas Valley Road (light). There is a gentle grade for about ½ miles, then a downhill to Freitas Parkway, just before the shopping center light (1½ miles).

Cross Freitas Parkway and bear left with the road. Continue past the shopping center. The road will turn into Los Ranchitos Road. Continue until the road comes to Highway 101. It goes uphill, gradually getting steeper.

Enter the bike path on the right. There is a narrow entrance in the chain-link fence. The path is short but *very steep*. Be prepared. Watch for other bicyclists coming down.

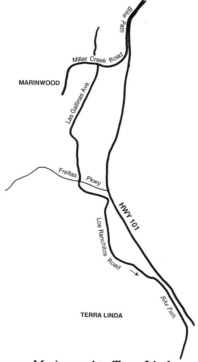

Marinwood to Terra Linda

Terra Linda to Corte Madera

Go up and over to Lincoln Avenue. Take Lincoln Avenue past downtown San Rafael to Irwin Street. for 2¼ miles. There is lots of traffic and lights. Turn right onto Irwin Street. Follow it up and over the hill. It turns into Tiburon Blvd. (totals about 1 mile).

Turn right onto Via La Cumbre. There is a *steep*, windy downhill. *Use caution!* Take a quick left on Eliseo Drive to Sir Francis Drake Blvd. (light). Turn left on Sir Francis Drake Blvd. A short distance on the right is the entrance to the bike path (just past Zim's restaurant) as a cut-out in sidewalk. Go under the freeway bridge to a boardwalk.

Follow the bike path around in half-circle to head west, away from the freeway. The bike path here follows Corte Madera Creek and ends on South Eliseo Drive. Continue straight to Bon Air. Turn left onto Bon Air, then turn left onto Magnolia (at the light). There is a bike path on the left side of the street so you can avoid the traffic. Turn left onto Doherty Drive, left on Lucky Drive, and right on Fifer Avenue (there is no sign). Just before the freeway, turn right and get onto Tamal Vista Blvd.

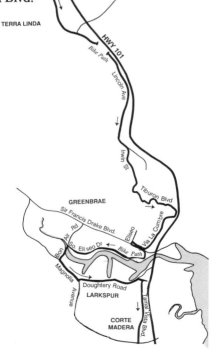

Terra Linda to Corte Madera

Corte Madera to Sausalito

Continue straight where the road turns into Madera Blvd. Cross Tamalpais Drive (light) and turn left onto Casa Buena Drive, which bears right to follow the freeway. Continue uphill (two short climbs) to the bike path. The entrance to the bike path is located at the top of the second climb; where the road makes a sharp, uphill climb turn to the right.

Take the bike path, which parallels Highway 101 and ends on Lomita Drive. Follow Lomita west (it turns right) to East Blithedale Avenue, until it rejoins the bike path. Watch for the wooden pole dividing the entrance to the bike path. This path will turn toward the left and rise uphill slightly to join the main path. Across East Blithedale is the bike path.

Continue across East Blithedale (at the light) and continue the bike path. It will take you out past Richardson Bay and underneath Highway 101. The bike path parallels the east side of Highway 101 and merges with Bridgeway Avenue. (This ride is more fully described in Ride No. 2: Mill Valley to Sausalito.)

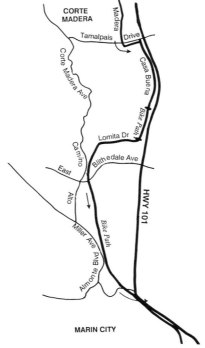

Corte Madera to Sausalito

Sausalito to the Golden Gate Bridge

Continue on Bridgeway. Turn left at Harbor Drive, then right onto Marinship Way. Continue until it rejoins Bridgeway, which will lead you into downtown Sausalito.

Continue on Bridgeway (traffic!) until it makes a sharp right turn. The road turns into Richardson. Take an immediate left onto Second Street (hill). Turn left onto South Street. At the top of the hill, the road turns to the right and becomes Alexander Drive. Turn left onto East Road into U.S. Army Reserve Center (Fort Baker). Watch for traffic when making your left turn!

Wind downhill, past the fishing pier, and ultimately go underneath Golden Gate Bridge. Continue uphill on the west side of the bridge to the entrance of the parking lot. You can now cross the bridge at this point.

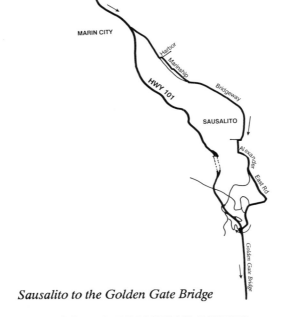

Sausalito to the Golden Gate Bridge

SOUTH ACCESS ALTERNATE ROUTES

#1: Petaluma to Novato (the long, scenic tour)

This alternate route is much longer and more scenic than using Highway 101, but it takes you through some spectacular country. Take "D" Street west out of town. Continue over Red Hill and then left onto Novato Blvd. (8 miles from the Petaluma city limits).

Continue to the intersection of San Marin Drive (on the left), Sutro Road (on the left) and Novato Blvd. at the stop sign (6 miles). Turn right onto Sutro Road, then left onto Center Road for about ¼-mile (it bypasses busy Novato Blvd.). Turn right at Diablo Avenue (1 mile), then left onto Hill Road ("T" with Diablo). Bear right onto Valley then bear left onto Arthur Street. Turn right onto Cambridge Street. Continue the rest of the ride as described.

#2: Larkspur Landing to Mill Valley

Take the bike path off Sir Francis Drake underneath Highway 101. It gets onto a wooden boardwalk. At the end of the boardwalk turn left toward the freeway. (A right turn leads toward Larkspur Landing and the Larkspur ferry terminal.)

The paved path ends at a narrow sidewalk alongside the freeway exit ramp. There is an opening in the concrete fence. Go left. It is recommended that you walk your bike. Exit sidewalk to the left at a similar opening in the concrete fence on the other side. Follow the path a short distance to Paradise Drive.

Cross the freeway at Tamalpais Drive, either by riding over the overpass or walking your bike on the pedestrian walk over. Turn left onto Casa Buena and continue as before to the bike lane.

#3: Corte Madera to Mill Valley

Continue along Magnolia past Doherty Drive. At Tamalpais Drive the road becomes Corte Madera Avenue, and then turns into Camino Alto. This is very pretty, but is steep, winding and narrow. Turn left onto East Blithedale and then right onto the bike path at Lomita Drive.

SOUTH TO NORTH ACCESS ROUTE
The Golden Gate Bridge to Novato

Begin your ride at the Vista parking lot at the east side of the Golden Gate Bridge. *Reverse the north-to-south route until you reach San Rafael.*

Alternate route: San Rafael to Novato

From San Pedro Road turn left at the Civic Center onto Civic Center Drive. (There are two lanes of traffic. USE CAUTION!) This road travels on the east side of the freeway and meets Smith Ranch Road (2 miles, at the stop sign). Turn left onto Smith Ranch Road and go under the freeway. The road becomes Lucas Valley Road. Continue to Las Galinas Avenue. Turn right onto Las Galinas. The rest of the ride is the reverse of the south route.

APPENDIX

Samuel P. Taylor State Park

RIDES BY RATINGS

EASY RIDES
(short rides, easy grades, good for beginners and children)

MEDIUM RIDES
(longer rides, some hills, not too strenuous)

CHALLENGING RIDES

(extensive rides with strenuous grades, for more experienced cyclists)

MOUNTAIN BIKE RIDES

BICYCLE SHOPS IN MARIN COUNTY

A Bicycle Odyssey
301 Caledonia
Sausalito, CA 94965
(415) 332-3050

Bike Hut
459 Entrada Drive
Novato, CA 94947
(415) 883-2440

Caesar's Cyclery
40 Greenfield Avenue
San Anselmo, CA 94960
(415) 258-9920

Corte Madera Cyclery
5629-5631 Paradise Drive
Corte Madera, CA 94525
(415) 924-3683

Cycle Dynamics
1531-B South Novato Blvd.
Novato, CA 94947
(415) 892-7342

Far-Go Bike Shops
191-B San Marin Plaza
Novato, CA 94947
(415) 897-0252

Far-Go Bike Shops
186 Northgate #1 Center
San Rafael, CA 94903
(415) 472-0253

Fisher Mountain Bikes
1501 San Anselmo Avenue
San Anselmo, CA 94960
(415) 459-2247

Fleet Feet Triathlete
1320 4th Street
San Rafael, CA 94901
(415) 456-1095

Ken's Bike & Sport
94 Main Street
Tiburon, CA 94920
(415) 435-1683

Mike's Bicycle Center
1601 4th Street
San Rafael, CA 94901
(415) 454-3747

Mill Valley Cyclery
369-371 Miller Avenue
mill Valley, CA 94941
(415) 388-6774

Novato Cyclery
871 Grant Avenue
Novato, CA 94947
(415) 892-5538

Planeaway
707 Sir Francis Drake Blvd.
San Anselmo, CA 94960
(415) 456-4950

Planeaway
1 Blackfield Drive
Tiburon, CA 94920
(415) 383-2123

Pt. Reyes Bikes
11431 State Route Hwy 1
Pt. Reyes Station, CA 94965
(415) 663-1768

Sausalito Cyclery
#1 Gate 6 Road
Sausalito, CA 94965
(415) 332-3200

Sunshine Bicycle Works
737 Center Blvd.
Fairfax, CA 94930
(415) 459-3334

Village Peddler
1141 Magnolia Avenue
Larkspur, CA 94939
(415) 461-3091

ANNUAL BICYCLING EVENTS

Marin Century   *(Early August)*

A challenging 100-mile ride, hosted by Marin Cyclists, that hits two of the three northern Marin sustained climbs: the Marshall Wall and Red Hill. The Century begins at Marin Civic Center in San Rafael and heads out to northern Marin via Lucas Valley and Nicasio. Riders roll past the Marin Cheese Factory and west over the Marshall Wall to the coast, where they head north to Valley Ford over rolling hills. Another 20 miles bring riders to Petaluma and the last rest stop before heading over Red Hill and back to San Rafael.

Pumpkin Century   *(Near Halloween)*

This is a no-fee, no rest stop, no sag, unpublished Century that is a favorite of club riders. The ride starts in Nicasio at 8 a.m. and works up through some of Marin's prettiest farming and dairy county into Sonoma and Valley Ford, which is a bail-out for those who don't want to continue the full 100 miles. Those who do ride north to Occidental and blast down Bohemian Highway to Duncan Mills and lunch. Back on the bike riders head south at the coast and blast through Bodega Bay back to Valley Ford. From there it's about 25 miles of rolling hills down the coast through Marshall to Point Reyes-Petaluma Road, just north of Pt. Reyes Station. Another 5 miles around Nicasio Reservoir brings the ride back to the Nicasio.

Turkey Day Road/Mountain Bike Rides   *(Thanksgiving Day)*

On Thanksgiving Day morning hundreds of local cyclists gather to burn calories on the road or on the mountain in preparation for guilt-free feasting later in the day.

Turkey Day Road Ride — This strenuous 50-mile loop begins at 9:30 a.m. at Tamalpais High School in Mill Valley. Riders immediately climb over Mount Tamalpais to Stinson Beach, then north to Olema where the pack turns east on Sir Francis Drake for the return to Fairfax and, eventually, Mill Valley.

Turkey Day Mountain Bike Ride — The Pine Mountain Loop is one of the most challenging rides for mountain bikers in Marin County. The ride begins at the Fairfax Theater parking lot and heads up Bolinas Road to Azalea Hill and the San Geronimo Ridge Road where the ride hits dirt. Following are some heart-stopping climbs and spectacular views before the route descends into the Kent Lake watershed, returning along San Geronimo Ridge to Repack Road and back down to Fairfax.

Written by Jeff Dooley

CALENDAR OF EVENTS

The following annual events are listed so that you can coordinate your bicycle trips with what's happening in Marin County.

JANUARY

POINT REYES NATIONAL SEASHORE

Whale Watching. California gray whales migrate south to Baja. Vista points are Point Reyes National Seashore, Marin Headlands and Lighthouse. January through April.

SAN RAFAEL

American Indian Traders. American Indian artists and traders from across the United States gather to display and sell traditional arts and crafts. Third weekend in January.

SAN RAFAEL

BAEER Fair. Exhibits and workshops promote awareness of the environment. Last Saturday in January.

FEBRUARY

SAN RAFAEL

American Indian Antique Art Show and Sale. Marin Civic Center. Third weekend in February.

MARCH

STINSON BEACH

Egret and Blue Heron Nesting Season. A rare glimpse of these majestic birds at home. Audubon Canyon Ranch. March-May.

APRIL

POINT REYES NATIONAL SEASHORE

Coastal Native American Spring Festival. Traditional dancing and songs. Bear Valley Headquarters.

SAUSALITO/ TIBURON

Opening of Yacht Season. Pleasure craft are decorated and blessed at this colorful celebration. Last Sunday in April.

TIBURON

Jazz Festival. Traditional New Orleans and Chicago jazz. Main Street. Third weekend in April.

MAY

MILL VALLEY

Mt. Tamalpais Mountain Plays. Annual production at the Mountain Theater. Six weekends in May and June.

MILL VALLEY	*Mill Valley Weekend.* Downtown sidewalk sale, artist's studio tours, history walk, parade and Afternoon in the Park. Memorial Day Weekend.
SAN RAFAEL	*Greek Festival.* Greek dancing, food and entertainment. Marin Civic Center Exhibit Hall. Memorial Day weekend.
TIBURON	*Wine Festival.* Wine-tasting, music and food. Point Tiburon. Second Saturday in May.

JUNE

FAIRFAX	*Annual Festival.* Arts and crafts show, music and food. Fairfax Park on Bolinas Road Park. Second weekend in June.
MILL VALLEY	*Wine Tasting Festival.* Enjoy the wines of California's finest wineries as well as cheese and food. Fourth Sunday in June.
MILL VALLEY	*Dipsea Race.* Famous 7-mile handicapped footrace. Second Sunday in June.
NOVATO	*Art and Wine Festival.* Grant Avenue, Old Town Novato. Last weekend in June.
POINT REYES STATION	*4-H Western Weekend Parade.* A parade and BBQ sponsored by the Lions Club. Red Barn. First weekend in June.
SAN ANSELMO	*Art and Wine Festival.* Along San Anselmo Avenue. Mid-June.
SAUSALITO	*Humming Toadfish Festival.* Music, food, booth, Classic Yacht Show. Bay Model. Last Sunday in June.

JULY

CORTE MADERA	*Fourth of July Parade.* Art fair and entertainment. Corte Madera Park.
MARIN CITY	*Community Festival.* Arts and crafts booths, music, dance and entertainment. Manzanita Center. Fourth of July weekend.
SAN RAFAEL	*Marin County Fair.* Exhibits, carnival rides, games and musical entertainment. Marin County Fairgrounds. Five days in July.

Appendix

SAN RAFAEL	*Town Picnic.* Forest Meadows at Dominican College. Games, entertainment, food and parade. Second Sunday in July.
SAUSALITO	*Fourth of July Parade and Community Picnic.* Earl Dunphy Park.

AUGUST

NOVATO	*Renaissance Pleasure Faire.* Games, entertainment, food, arts and crafts. Six weekends in August and September.

SEPTEMBER

MILL VALLEY	*Fall Arts Festival.* Old Mill Park. Labor Day Weekend.
SAN ANSELMO	*Peddler's Fair.* Arts and crafts. Memorial Park. Last Saturday in September.
SAN ANSELMO	*Country Fair Days.* Town parade and other activities. Creek Park. Last Sunday in September.
SAUSALITO	*Arts and Crafts Festival.* Musical entertainment and refreshments. Vacant waterfront land off Bridgeway near Locust Avenue. Labor Day weekend.
TIBURON	*Chili Festival.* Chili-tasting, prizes, games for children. Bank of America parking lot. Second Saturday in September.

OCTOBER

LARKSPUR	*Sunnyhills Grape Festival.* Arts and crafts sale. Larkspur Landing. First Saturday in October.
PT. REYES NATIONAL SEASHORE	*Indian Festival.* Demonstrations of traditional crafts. Kule Loklo. Mid-October on Saturday.

DECEMBER

SAN ANSELMO	*Christmas Marketplace.* Crafts sales at the San Anselmo Recreation Center, 1000 Sir Francis Drake Blvd. First weekend of December.
SAN RAFAEL	*Festival of Trees.* Sales of holiday ornaments and baked goods. Marin Wildlife Center. First weekend in December.

POINTS OF INTEREST

The following points of interest are listed so that you can take advantage of some of what Marin County has to offer. Most are either free or charge a small fee.

Angel Island

Ferry to Angel Island
Main Street, Tiburon
(415) 546-2815

The 740-acre island is about 1 mile from Tiburon and was the site of a native Indian settlement, Civil War fort, U.S. troop embarkation site, and an immigration center from about 1910 to 1940. Many historic buildings remain. Picnic areas are available by the ferry landing at Ayala Cove. Hiking and biking trails circle the island. There are exhibits and slide show at Park Headquarters in the summer as well as special events.

Belvedere

China Cabin
52 Beach Road (off Tiburon Blvd.)
(415) 435-1853

The Social Saloon, commonly known as the China Cabin, was once the luxurious Victorian saloon of the *SS China*. In 1866, before the ship was retired and eventually burned for scrap metal, the Saloon was removed from the top deck, restored, and then barged over to Belvedere Cove. Today it serves as a maritime center for private functions and is recognized as a national maritime treasure. The Saloon is open to the public two days a week during the summer, or by appointment throughout the year.

Bolinas

The Point Reyes Bird Observatory
Mesa Road

Located on the Bolinas Mesa, the observatory is the only full-time ornithological research station in the United States.

Bolinas Memorial Museum
(415) 868-0330

This tiny museum will give you a lesson in Bolinas history. It specializes in collecting the personal memorabilia of local residents.

Corte Madera

Bay Area Discovery Museum
428 Corte Madera Town Center (at Tamalpais Drive)
(415) 927-4722

This unique hands-on museum is designed to help children learn about their environment. Exhibits include an architecture area with drafting equipment, a stage with costumes to try on, and a tunnel that simulates the sights and sounds under the Bay.

Golden Gate National Recreational Area
(Marin Headlands)

This 40,000-acre area is located just west of the Golden Gate Bridge. Some of the best views of San Francisco are from the bluffs of the Headlands. You will also find remnants of military bunkers. There are three forts in the Headlands — Baker, Cronkhite, and Barry. Wherever you go, bring along a jacket as the weather can change quite suddenly.

Battery Hill 129 (Hawk Hill)
Conzelman Road

This is the highest bluff where you can get the best view of the entire Bay Area and the Golden Gate Bridge. On a clear day you can see Mount Diablo, more than 30 miles to the east. It is nicknamed "Hawk Hill" because it is also one of the best places on the West Coast for watching the fall migration of hawks and other large birds of prey.

Golden Gate Raptor Observatory
Conzelman Road (at Hawk Hill)
(415) 331-0730

This center is quite active during the fall hawk migration. Organized hikes occur from 10 a.m. to 4 p.m. and banding demonstrations are scheduled on Sundays.

Golden Gate Youth Hostel
Building 941, Fort Barry
(415) 331-2777

Set in the heart of the Marin Headlands, the hostel is large and has a large kitchen, recreation room, fireplace and piano. It accommodates up to 60 guests at $6.50 per night. Opens 4:30 p.m.

Marin Mammal Center
Fort Cronkhite
331-SEAL (0161)

The Center rescues and treats sea lions, seals and other oceanic mammals in need of medical attention along California's coast until they are well enough to return to their natural environment. Open from 10 a.m. to 4 p.m. daily. Admission is free, but donations are appreciated.

Marin Headlands Visitors Center
Bunker Road, Fort Cronkhite
(415) 331-1540

A lovely place to visit where you can get books, maps and information about the Golden Gate National Recreation Area and vicinity.

Pacific Energy and Resources Center
Fort Cronkhite, Building 1055
(415) 332-8200

This non-profit organization provides educational programs in energy conservation and renewable energy resources, as well as an exhibit hall, a library and a children's learning center.

Point Bonita Lighthouse
(415) 331-1540

Built in 1877, the Point Bonita Lighthouse was one of the West Coast's first lighthouses. It offers magnificent views of Point Reyes to the north and San Francisco to the south. To get to the Lighthouse you walk through a tunnel and across a suspension bridge. Weekend hours are 12:30 to 4:00 p.m. Lighthouse tours begin at 1:00 p.m. Saturdays and Sundays, and are about an hour in length.

Marin Municipal Water District

Marin Municipal Water District Lakes
(415) 924-4600

A protected watershed on 20,000 acres of recreational land with is a system of five reservoirs: Phoenix, Bon Tempe, Lagunitas, Alpine and Kent. Here you can fish, hike, picnic, cycle and ride horseback.

Mill Valley

Muir Woods
Muir Woods Road
(415) 388-2595

This 550-acre preserve is an old-growth stand of giant coastal redwoods (Sequoia sempervirens), some over 200 feet in height There are 6 miles of self-guided marked paved hiking trails, including a braille trail for the blind. Be sure to bring a sweater; even on hots days the shade can be chilly. There is no picnicking or snacking allowed in the park. Open daily from 8 a.m. until sunset. Parking can be a problem at any time of year.

Mt. Tamalpais State Park

Mt. Tamalpais is often called the "Sleeping Maiden" because of the contours in the mountain. The summit is at 2,571 feet above sea level and was once lined with hotels and taverns. A scenic railway brought tourists up the mountain from Mill Valley. A fire destroyed most of the structures in 1929. From the top you can see a spectacular panorama of the entire Bay Area. There are a network of hiking, biking and horse trails for exploration. Open daily from 7 a.m. to sunset. Admission is free.

West Point Inn

One of the few remaining buildings, West Point Inn offers hikers and bicyclists a rest stop with refreshments and glorious views as well as inexpensive overnight accommodations. There is no access by car.

Sidney B. Cushing Memorial Theatre

The "Mountain Theater," as it is popularly called, is a beautiful natural stone amphitheater that was constructed by the Civilian Conservation Corps during the 1930s. The theater can seat up to 3,500 people and is a popular setting for weddings and special events, including the traditional Mountain Plays that have been held each spring since 1913.

Novato

Marin Community College/Indian Valley College Campus
1800 Ignacio Blvd exit off Hwy 101
(415) 883-2211

Set on 333 rolling acres, a small creek runs through the landscaped grounds. The pool and tennis courts are open to the public, and there is also an art gallery.

Marin French Cheese Company
7500 Point Reyes-Petaluma Road
(707) 762-6001

Manufacturer of French cheeses — Camembert, Brie, Breakfast and Schloss. Fifteen-minute tours are scheduled from 10:00 a.m. to 4:00 p.m. There is a picnic area, lagoon with piped-in background classical music, and picnic supplies. Open from 9 a.m. to 5 p.m.

Marin Museum of the American Indian
2200 Novato Blvd. (near San Marin Drive)
(415) 897-4064

The Museum gives a historic display about the Coast Miwok and Pomo Indians, who once lived in the area. Park facilities include hiking trails, picnic areas, and playing fields. Located in Miwok Park.

Novato History Museum
815 DeLong Avenue (at Reichert Street)
(415) 897-4320

This small museum features exhibits of historical photographs and displays illustrating the history of Novato.

Point Reyes National Seashore

This 65,000-acre park offers hiking and biking trails, campgrounds and beautiful vistas. The principal trailheads are Bear Valley, Palomarin, Five Brooks and Estero. All have adequate parking. Trail maps are available at any visitor center.

Bear Valley Visitors' Center
(415) 663-1092

The Visitors' Center, built in 1983, is housed in a 2,500 square foot barn-sized building. The Center has exhibits, a collection room for artifacts, a library, auditorium, and general information area, and is a great place to learn about the coastal area. Open Monday through Friday 9:00 a.m. to 5:00 p.m.; weekends and holidays 8 a.m. to 5:00 p.m.

Earthquake Trail

A paved .6-mile trail that runs along the San Andreas fracture zone of the famous 1906 earthquake. This self-guided walk includes exhibits of the damage caused by the 1906 quake and presents a clear story about earthquakes. Open seven days a week sunrise to sunset.

Ken Patrick Visitor Center

This Visitor Center is located at beautiful Drakes Beach. Displays and has displays about the Gulf of the Farallones National Marine Sanctuary, sea animals found within the area and an assortment of interesting shells. Open weekends and holidays 10:00 a.m. to 5:00 p.m.

Morgan Horse Ranch

Located 1/4-mile from the Bear Valley Visitor Center, this working horse ranch is where horses are trained for use by Park Rangers. Exhibits, corrals and demonstrations. Open seven days a week, 9:00 a.m. to 4:30 p.m.

Kule Loklo ("Bear Valley")

A replica of a Coast Miwok Indian Village. Built in 1976, cultural demonstrations and exhibits explain about the former residents of Point Reyes. The village is located 1.4 miles from the Bear Valley Visitor Center and is open seven days a week, sunrise to sunset.

Point Reyes Youth Hostel
(415) 663-8811

Set in a secluded valley, the hostel's rustic ranchhouse and bunkhouse include a spacious kitchen, an outdoor barbecue and patio, plus two common rooms with wood-burning stoves. This 44-bed hostel is open nightly to groups and individuals, and costs $6.50 per person per night. Opens 4:30 p.m.

Point Reyes Lighthouse
(415) 669-1534

The Lighthouse was built in 1870 to guide ships through the treacherous waters around Pt. Reyes. It became automated in 1975. To get to the lighthouse you must walk down a steep, 300-step stairway cut into the rugged cliff. On the way down to the Lighthouse you can see seals and sea lions on the beaches below.

The Lighthouse is a favorite place for whale watching. Gray whales can be spotted passing by the lighthouse on their way to Baja, California and Mexico during December and January. From mid-March through May they head back to the cold water in the Bering and Chukchi Seas.

San Anselmo

San Anselmo Historical Museum
110 Turnstead Avenue (at San Anselmo Avenue)
(415) 258-4666

This museum has exhibits about the railroad that cut through this area 100 years ago, the 1982 flood and other highlights of San Anselmo history. Located in the San Anselmo Public Library building.

San Geronimo

Samuel P. Taylor State Park
Sir Francis Drake Blvd.

Once the location of a paper and gunpowder mill constructed in the 1850's, the park contains 2,576 acres of redwood forests. There are miles of hiking, biking and equestrian trails as well as picnicking. There is swimming and fishing in Paper Mill Creek. Bike trails start at Platform Bridge on Sir Francis Drake Blvd. and at the Park entrance. Special campsites, at reduced fees, are set aside for bikers and backpackers. Reservations for these campsites may be made through Ticketron.

San Rafael

China Camp Village
North San Pedro Road

China Camp was one of twenty or thirty Chinese fishing villages that once dotted the shore of San Francisco Bay where they would harvest local grass shrimp. A museum displays the remains of Chinese immigrants' fishing camp.

China Camp State Park
North San Pedro Road
(415) 456-0766 or 426-1286

This 1,640-acre park lies on the southeast shores of San Pablo Bay was once a Chinese fishing village. It has a variety of natural scenery and a network of hiking and biking trails along San Pablo Ridge with magnificent views of the San Pablo Bay Area. There are primitive campsites. The 1900 general store is now a museum. Day use parking fee is $3.00.

Farmer's Market
Marin County Civic Center Fairgrounds
Civic Center Drive (off San Pedro Road)
(415) 456-3276

Held in the parking lot of the Marin Veteran's Memorial Auditorium, this market offers the freshest produce, ranch eggs, herbs, honey, nuts, flowers, plants, local fish and breads. Open Thursdays, from 8:00 a.m. to 1:00 p.m., and Sundays, from 9:00 a.m. to 2 p.m., rain or shine.

Marin County Civic Center
30 North San Pedro Road (off Hwy 101)
(415) 472-7470

This blue-domed complex was designed by Frank Lloyd Wright in 1958, and houses Marin County offices, the Hall of Justice and the Library. Many architectural designs were used in the Hall of Justice. A large skylight allows natural light into the lush indoor gardens. Tours are given Monday through Friday 9:00 a.m to 3:00 p.m. by appointment.

Marin County Historical Society Museum
Boyd Park
1125 B Street (at Mission Street)
(415) 454-8538

This museum features exhibits devoted to Louise Boyd, the last heiress of the Boyd estate. The collection of memorabilia includes some of her crystal photographs.

Marin Wildlife Center
76 Albert Park Lane (at B Street)
(415) 454-6961

This wild animal refuge serves as an emergency room for sick or injured wildlife. Tours of the facilities can be arranged, and adult and family hikes are offered.

Mission San Rafael Archangel
1104 5th Avenue (between Court Street and B Street)
(415) 454-8141

Established in 1817 by the Spanish Franciscan friars, this mission was also inhabited by the Marin Miwok Indians. There is a collection of historical artifacts of the mission's history. Mass is still celebrated here daily.

Sausalito

San Francisco Bay Delta Model
2100 Bridgeway Drive at Spring Street
(415 332-3871

The Bay Model is a hydraulic working scale model used to analyze the entire San Francisco Bay Delta areas in characteristics and behavior. Housed in a 1½-acre warehouse near Sausalito, the building was originally constructed in 1942 for producing World War II Liberty ships. Self-guided tours. Open 10 a.m. to 4 p.m. Tuesday through Friday, 9 a.m. to 4 p.m. Saturday. Admission is free.

Stinson Beach

Audubon Canyon Ranch
4900 Hwy 1 (3 miles north of Stinson Beach)
(415) 868-9244

This 1,000-acre ranch was named in honor of John James Audubon and is a wildlife sanctuary and nature education center. There is a picnic area, a bookstore and museum, and you can observe the Great Blue Heron and Great Egret nesting colony from the hiking trails on the park grounds. Open weekends and holidays March 1 through July 4 from 10 a.m. to 4 p.m. Admission is free.

Slide Ranch
Shoreline Highway (between Muir Beach and Stinson Beach)
(415) 381-6155

Slide Ranch is a unique demonstration farm where visitors can watch workers milk goats, shear sheep, pick vegetables, and even slaughter chickens. There is no charge to walk around the 164 acres of ranch property, which has hiking trails and tide pools..

Steep Ravine Environmental Campground
Shoreline Highway (2 miles south of Stinson Beach)
(800) 952-5580

This campground is owned by Mount Tamalpais State Park and features ten rustic cabins and six primitive campsites. Primitive toilets, water faucets, and firewood are nearby. Reservations are recommended.

Tiburon

National Audubon Society/
Richardson Bay Audubon Center
376 Greenwood Beach Road (off Tiburon Blvd.)
(415) 388-2524

From October through March, the Sanctuary acts as a refuge for many thousands of waterfowl and shore birds that migrate to the Bay. There is a self-guiding nature trail that overlooks Richardson Bay and San Francisco. Open to the public Wednesday through Sunday from 9:00 a.m. to 5:00 p.m.

Lyford House

A Victorian home located on the grounds of the National Audubon Society, offers tours and occasional art exhibits. Built in 1876 on Strawberry Point by Dr. and Mrs. Benjamin Lyford after a visit to the Philadelphia Expo of 1876, it was barged to its present site in 1957. Open to the public 1:00 to 4:00 p.m. Sundays during the school year.

Old St. Hilary's Historic Preserve
Esperanza Street and Mar West Street
(415) 435-1853

One of the few examples of a Carpenter's Gothic church in California left in its original condition and setting. Because of the elegant woodwork and intimate space it is often used as a setting for weddings, chamber music, memorial services and other   events. Open to the public Wednesday and Sunday 1:00 to 4:00 p.m., April to October.

Tomales

Tomales Bay State Park
4 miles north of Inverness
(415) 669-1140

This 1,018-acre park across Tomales Bay offers swimming beaches, fishing, hiking and picnic areas. Another part of the park is on the opposite shore of Tomales Bay is at Millerton Point, located on a shallow bay with picnic tables, fire pits, restrooms, and swimming beach. There is a bike camp (fee).

CALIFORNIA BICYCLE LAWS

The following are excerpts taken from the 1987 California Vehicle Code relating to the operation and equipping of bicycles. Some of the sections of the laws listed have been reworded slightly and/or abbreviated.

RIGHTS AND RESPONSIBILITIES 21200

A. Every person riding a bicycle upon a highway has all the rights and is subject to all the provisions applicable to the driver of a motor vehicle, including stopping at stop signs, traveling in the same direction as motorists, granting right-of-way to pedestrians and vehicles, and obeying traffic signals.

B. *Riding Under the Influence of Alcohol or Drugs* 21200.5
It is unlawful for any person to ride a bicycle upon a highway while under the influence of an alcoholic beverage or any drug, or under the combined influence of an alcoholic beverage and any drug A conviction of a violation shall be punished by a fine of not more than two hundred fifty dollars ($250).

EQUIPMENT REQUIREMENTS 21201

A. *Brakes* — No person shall operate a bicycle on a roadway unless it is equipped with a brake which will enable the operator to make one braked wheel skid on dry, level, clean pavement.

B. *Handlebars* — No person shall operate on the highway any bicycle equipped with handlebars so raised that the operator must elevate his hands above the level of his shoulders in order to grasp the normal steering grip area.

C. *Bicycle Size* — No person shall operate upon any highway a bicycle which is of such a size as to prevent the operator from safely stopping the bicycle, supporting it in an upright position with at least one foot on the ground, and restarting it in a safe manner.

D. *Lights and Reflectors* — Every bicycle operated upon any highway during darkness shall be equipped with:

1. a lamp emitting a white light which, while the bicycle is in motion, illuminates the highway in front of the bicyclist and is visible from a distance of 300 feet in front and from the sides of the bicycle.

2. a red reflector visible from a distance of 500 feet to the rear.

3. a white or yellow reflector mounted on each pedal visible from the front and rear of the bicycle from a distance of 200 feet.

4. a white or yellow reflector on each side forward of the center of the bicycle, and a white or red reflector on each side to the rear of the center of the bicycle, except that bicycles which are equipped with reflectorized tires on the front and rear need not be equipped with these side reflectors.

OPERATION ON ROADWAY   21202

A. *Two-way Street* — Any person operating a bicycle upon a roadway at a speed less than the normal speed of traffic moving in the same direction at such time shall ride as close as practicable to the right-hand curb or edge of the roadway except:

1. when overtaking and passing another bicycle or motor vehicle proceeding in the same direction.

2. when preparing for a left turn at an intersection or into a private road or driveway.

3. when reasonably necessary to avoid conditions (including, but not limited to, fixed or moving objects, vehicles, bicycles, pedestrians, animals, surface hazards, or substandard width lanes) that make it unsafe to continue along the right-hand curb or edge.

B. *One-Way Street* — Any person operating a bicycle upon a roadway, which carries traffic in one direction only has two or more marked traffic lanes may ride as near the left-hand curb or edge of such roadway as practicable; however, this is the only situation in which you may do so.

HITCHING RIDES   21203

No person riding upon a bicycle shall attach the bicycle or himself to any streetcar or vehicle on the roadway.

RIDING ON BICYCLE   21204

A. No person operating a bicycle upon a highway shall ride other than upon or astride a permanent and regular attached seat.

B. No operator shall allow a person riding as a passenger, and no person shall ride as a passenger, on a bicycle upon a highway other than upon or astride a separate attached seat. If the passenger is four years of age or younger, or weighs 40 pounds or less, the seat shall have adequate provision for retaining the passenger in place and for protecting the passenger from moving parts of the bicycle.

C. No person operating a bicycle upon a highway shall allow any person who is four years of age or younger, or weighs 40 pounds or less, to ride as a passenger on a bicycle unless that passenger is wearing a helmet meeting the standards of the American National Standards Institute (ANSI Z 90.4 bicycle helmet standards) or of the Snell Memorial Foundation's 1984 Standard for Protective Headgear for Use in Bicycling.

D. Wearing a helmet means having a helmet of good fit fastened securely upon the head with the helmet straps.

CARRYING ARTICLES   21205

No person operating a bicycle shall carry any package, bundle, or article which prevents the operator from keeping at least one hand upon the handlebars.

BICYCLE LANES   21208

A. Whenever a bicycle lane has been established on a roadway, any person operating a bicycle upon the roadway at a speed less than the normal speed of traffic moving in the same direction shall ride within the bicycle lane, except:

1. when overtaking and passing another bicycle, vehicle, or pedestrian within the lane or about to enter the lane if such overtaking and passing cannot be done safely within the lane.

2. when preparing for a left turn at an intersection or into a private road or driveway.

3. when reasonably necessary to leave the bicycle lane to avoid debris or other hazardous conditions.

B. No person operating a bicycle shall leave a bicycle lane until the movement can be made with reasonable safety and then only after giving an appropriate signal in the event that any vehicle may be affected by the movement.

BICYCLE PARKING 21210

No person shall leave a bicycle lying on its side on any sidewalk, or shall park a bicycle on a sidewalk in any other position, so that there is not an adequate path for pedestrian traffic.

FREEWAYS 21960

A. The Department of Transportation and local authorities may prohibit or restrict the use of the freeways or any portion thereof by pedestrians, bicycles or other nonmotorized traffic or by any person operating a motor-driven cycle or a motorized bicycle.

B. Such prohibitory regulation shall be effective when appropriate signs giving notice thereof are erected upon any freeway and the approaches thereto.

HAND SIGNALS 22111

All required signals given by hand and arm shall be given in the following manner:

Left Turn — hand and arm extended horizontally beyond the left side of the bicycle.

Right Turn — hand and arm extended upward beyond the left side of the bicycle, or right hand and arm extended horizontally to the right side of the bicycle [not recommended].

Stop or sudden decrease of speed — hand and arm extended downward beyond the left side of the bicycle.

BICYCLING TIPS

With the emphasis on fitness and exercise bicycling has once again taken off as one of the enjoyable sports of all time. Understanding your bicycle and its limitations are essential in preparing yourself for an enjoyable outing.

GENERAL RULES OF THE ROAD

1. *Keep to the right and move with the flow of traffic.* Riding on the left against traffic increases the chance for accidents because the force of collision is greater. Riding the wrong way is a leading cause of accidents between bicycle and motorist. Only pedestrians are permitted to travel facing oncoming traffic.

2. *Ride in single file off to the right side of the road.*

3. *Signal your moves so that motorists know what you intend to do.* Use the correct hand signals (see California Bicycle Laws).

4. *Never ride on freeways, toll roads, or major highways.* At those high speeds you could become severely injured or killed. Highway shoulders are frequently littered with broken glass and other hazardous debris. Avoid congested streets and use bike paths and lanes wherever possible.

5. *Watch out for soft or uneven shoulders and other road surface hazards.* You could easily skid and slip out into the road. When riding on dirt roads be very careful and slow down before turning corners. You could skid on sandy or gravel surfaces.

6. *Cross railroad tracks at a right angle (head-on).* When they are wet, walk your bicycle across them.

7. *Avoid riding in the rain.* Wet brakes and pavement can more than double your stopping distance and can cause a serious skid as well. The slippery surface and impaired visibility make riding in the rain a real hazard. Dry out your brakes after going through water by braking slightly for a short distance.

8. *Don't ride at night without headlights, taillights and reflectors on your bike* (see California Bicycle Laws). Also, wear reflectorized tape on your clothes or wear a reflective vest or jacket.

9. *Watch out for child cyclists.* Children on bicycles tend to weave from side to side, turn unpredictably without signaling, and may even collide with you when you are trying to pass them.

10. *In general, drive your bicycle defensively! Watch out for the other guy! Know your right of way, but don't insist upon it.* Remember that motorists often do not see bicycles, or even remember to watch out for them. Leave yourself enough room to take quick defensive action.

Bicycling in the City

1. *When traveling straight keep to the right.* Look behind to check on traffic more frequently.

2. *Don't do anything unpredictable,* like stopping suddenly, without having made sure nobody is following so closely as to be endangered.

3. *Keep your hands on or near the brake levers at all times* so that you can stop instantly if you have to. Keep your toe straps loose.

4. *Never ride on sidewalks unless special signs indicate that bicycles are permitted.*

5. *Watch out for doors of parked cars opening ahead of you, or for cars pulling out into traffic.* Motorists forget to watch for bicycles, so cyclists had better watch out for them.

6. *Be extremely careful at intersections.* That's where most accidents happen. Watch out for cars making a turn across your path. If traffic is heavy, walk your bike with pedestrian traffic; use the crosswalks.

7. *Leave enough room for others to overtake you whenever possible without endangering yourself.*

8. *Watch out for potholes and driveway curbs.* Touring bike wheels are very delicate and you may damage your tire or rim if you hit one. You may also wind up on the ground. You can avoid some damage to your bike by raising yourself off the saddle momentarily, if the hole or curb cannot be avoided.

9. *Watch out for drainage grates.* Those facing your direction can catch your wheel, forcing it into an abrupt stop and sending you flying over the handlebars.

10. *Don't turn left without first having made sure the road is clear behind you,* giving a clear signal and moving over to the center of the road (or to a left-turn lane) well ahead of your actual turn.

11. *Watch for approaching road users coming the other way and crossing or turning traffic coming from side roads.* Ride far

enough out into the road to keep an eye out for crossing traffic. Look well ahead, and scan the edge of the road for clues to the unexpected, such as car doors opening, pedestrians stepping out, cars ahead of you turning off or pulling up.

12. *In general, look ahead, think ahead, and use the skill you developed as a motorist, so you will be safe as a bicyclist too.*

Bicycle Touring

1. *When touring long distances, both you and your bicycle should be in good condition.*

2. *Carry spare parts with you,* such as simple repair tools, a patch kit or spare tube, and a bicycle pump.

3. *Never begin a trip on an empty stomach.* Eat *before* becoming hungry; drink *before* becoming thirsty. Take a water bottle with you. Carry some quick energy foods, such as a candy bar or fruit to snap you back and supply you with renewed energy. A banana will not only fill you up but is an excellent source of potassium.

4. *Stay in single file when riding with others.* Wait for the slower ones to catch up.

5. *Don't follow too closely behind.* You may not be able to avoid a pot-hole, obstacle, or a fallen cyclist in time. Be sure that you can see far enough ahead to brake safely.

Off-Road Bicycling

Off-road bicycling has become a challenging, new sport where bicycles are now riding on dirt roads and rugged terrain once only accessible to hikers and equestrians.

1. *Wear a helmet at all times as well as protective clothing, including eye protection and biking gloves.*

2. *Carry with you sufficient drinking water, a tire pump, a spare tub or patch kit, tire irons, special tools and an adjustable wrench.*

3. *Have an understanding of your personal ability and equipment, and prepared for the unexpected.* Your needs will differ, depending on where you ride and the type of riding you do. Be prepared and equipped to look after yourself and your bike.

4. *Plan ahead.* Each ride should be determined by your ability and equipment, the terrain and weather conditions.

5. *If you ride alone,* leave word with someone regarding where you plan to go, your route and anticipated time of return.

6. *Look ahead and anticipate any hazards in your path.* Evaluate the road or trail surface ahead of you, to pick out in advance the kind of obstacles that will be likely to stop your front wheel — deep chuckholes and high ridges, ditches, trees, logs and large rocks.

7. *Try to anticipate where somebody or something might appear suddenly,* such as pedestrians, cyclists, motorists, children or animals. Also, consider the liability factor involved in any impact you may have on *them.*

8. *Before starting out, check your seat height and your tire pressure.* Experiment with both. A quick-relase seat bolt will allow you to adjust your seat height easily on the trail. You can tailor it as you go.

9. *Don't over-inflate your tires.* You will lose traction. Most off-road tires have a suggested high and low tire pressure marked on the side For off-road bicycling, use the lower suggested pressure.

10. *When riding down hills lower your seat a little.* This will lower your center of gravity and keep your seat out of your way so that you can stand up and shift your body weight forward and backward over each bump.

11. *Maintain a comfortable steady pace, increasing your speed slightly as you climb a hill.* Select a comfortable gear and then gear down one; you can always gear up, if necessary.

Off-Road Riding in Marin County Parks

When using the Marin County Park System it is important to know the park regulations for bicycles. Check with a ranger or other official regarding the current status of bicycle regulations on the land you plan to ride.

1. *Stay on designated bike trails.* Bicycles are not permitted on many hiking trails. *There is a fine for violating this regulation.*

2. *Avoid practices that contribute to erosion.* Avoid muddy sections, excessive braking or skidding and cross-country routes. Don't trample native vegetation.

3. *Don't disturb wildlife.* Give them time to move away from your path.

4. *Pack out litter.* If you have room, pack out more than your share.

5. *Slow down and pass with care.* The maximum speed for all vehicles is 15 miles per hour. At blind turns and when passing others 5 miles per hour is required.

6. *Slow your speed and anticipate switchbacks and curves cautiously.* A hiker or horse may be approaching just around the bend.

7. *Be careful not to startle or interfere with hikers or horses on the trail.* Pass with care by letting others know of your presence well in advance by ringing a handlebar bell or with a greeting, "On your left (or right)."

8. *Always yield to hikers and equestrians.* If necessary, dismount your bicycle and wait for them to pass or signal you to pass. Be especially careful when approaching a horse. A skittish one may shy at an unfamiliar object, such as a bicycle, and kick out or run away, endangering its rider and/or anyone in its path.

9. Abide by the code of the responsible off-road bicyclist: *Take only pictures; leave only knobby prints.*

CLOTHING

1. *Always wear a bicycle helmet* to minimize the effects of a possible head injury in case of a bicycle traffic accident or just falling off your bike. About 50-75 percent of all bicycling fatalities can be directly attributed to head injury. Bicycling helmets provide a cushioning effect in a fall. Make sure that your helmet is especially designed for biking and meets the ANSI Z90.4 or Snell standards.

2. *Clothing worn on any bicycle trip should be brightly colored* (suggested colors are yellow, orange, and white). To make sure you can be seen in the dark, wear reflective tape on your clothes, or wear a reflective vest or jacket. Don't wear loose clothes that can get caught in the pedals or wheels.

3. *Biking clothes are usually made of polypropelene or Lycra and are aeronomically designed to reduce wind resistance.*

   • Shorts provide maximum comfort in warm weather. In cooler weather long cycling tights are comfortable and safe to wear. Not only are they padded, but, because they stretch they won't restrict your movements.

   • Jackets are designed to protect you from wind reistance in front but are ventilated in back against heat build-up.

Appendix

- Jerseys are made of fabric that keeps you warm against sweat and can breathe. They also provide deep back pockets for snacks and money.

4. *When wearing long pants wear a leg clip or band on your right leg* (preferable wear one on each leg) to keep the pants away from the chain. Also consider wearing biking underwear under regular pants.

5. *Wear shoes at all times* to avoid getting your toes caught in moving parts. Biking shoes are made stiffer to give you better support than standard shoes and are more efficient.

6. *Wear biking gloves on long rides.* The padding will protect your hands from constant pressure to the palms, which might cause temporary nerve damage and will also protect your hands if you fall. Without padding to protect your palms your hands will become numb and could eventually contract carpal tunnel syndrome. To prevent this shift your hand position often and keep your elbows bent and shoulders relaxed.

BICYCLE EQUIPMENT

1. *Make sure that your bicycle is the right size for you.* One that is too large or too small will be more difficult to control and uncomfortable to ride. To measure your bike, straddle the top tube of the frame with both feet flat on the ground. You should have 1 to 2 inches of clearance and be able to mount and dismount easily.

2. *Adjust the saddle to the correct height.* A saddle that is placed too low can cause fatigue and discomfort, and can considerably reduce your riding efficiency. Raise the saddle until your bare heel, placed on the pedal in its lowest position, is almost fully extended without your knees locking in place.

3. *Toe clips are highly recommended* because they let your muscles pull up as well push down on the pedals. Keep them loose when you're just learning to use them and when you're riding on city streets.

Shifting

1. *Understand your gear shift controls.* Shifting into the wrong gear can not only wear parts, but can also make you lose control of your bicycle (see page 126).

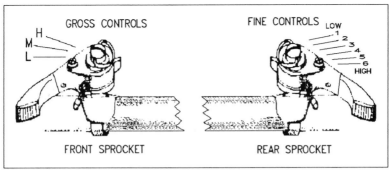

Gear-Shift Levers (18 speeds)

2. *Shift when pedaling becomes too difficult or too easy.* Try to maintain a steady pace.

3. *When making any gear changes keep the pedals moving.* Never change gears when not in motion.

4. *Avoid cross-chaining your gears* (using the small front chain ring and small rear sprocket, and large front chain ring and large back chain ring) This is especially bad with triple front chain rings which are common on mountain bikes. They put stress on the derailleur and tend to stretch the chain.

5. *Shift to a lower gear before you reach an upgrade.* Otherwise you will put too much strain on the gears and the chain.

6. *The gear-shift levers* should be moved slowly, until a solid "clicking" sound is heard. Any chattering or scraping sounds can be cleared by slight lever movement. Newer bikes have "index" shifters which make shifting much easier.

7. *When approaching a stop, move your left gear shift lever to the low range.* That way you don't have to pedal so hard when you first start up.

Braking

1. *When braking on the straight-away, use the rear brake first, followed by the front brake.* Exception: in loose gravel or on a slippery surface, use only the rear brake. Avoid using the front brake alone. It can send you flying over the handlebars.

2. *When braking in an emergency situation, shift your body weight toward the rear of the bicycle.*

Bicycle Maintenance

1. *Drive a safe bicycle. Make sure it is in good mechanical condition.* Oil squeaks and moving parts, adjust gears and brakes, check tire pressure, and tighten nuts and bolts periodically.

2. *Never back up your bike or pedal backwards.* Derailleurs are not designed for going backwards and may become damaged.

3. *Never sit on your bicycle with the kickstand down.* You can put considerable stress on the frame and damage it.

4. *Avoid getting water or sand into the rear wheel.* It can damage the gears, chain and bearings. If you do get sand on your bicycle be sure to wash it off at the earliest opportunity.

5. *Keep your tires at full pressure.* Use a bicycle tire pump. Service station pumps use 185 pounds of pressure and may inflate your tire too fast with too much pressure, and could cause a blowout. Their gauges may also be inaccurate. If you must use a service station pump, inflate your tire in short spurts and carry your own pressure gauge. (You might consider equipping your bike with heavy-duty inner tubes or tire protectors to help avoid flats.)

6. *Always lock your bicycle when it is going to be left unattended for any length of time.* Use a strong, case-hardened steel chain or cable and heavy-duty lock. Kryptonite locks, though bulky, are virtually theft-proof. Secure the chain through both wheels *and* frame, not just through the wheel, and then around a stationary object, such as a bike rack, tree or post.

7. *Store your bicycle with both gear shift levers in such a position as to leave the cables relaxed.*

ABOUT THE AUTHOR

Phyllis Neumann is a Marriage and Family Counselor and has a private practive in Petaluma. She enjoys computers, writing, bicycling and skiing. At this time she writes a Family Counselor column for the *Petaluma Post*. She is also the newsletter editor for the IBM PC Users Group of the Redwoods in Santa Rosa.

Her first book, *Sonoma County Bike Trails,* was published in 1978 and has been updated and printed each year. The book continues to be popular and sell well in and around the Bay Area.

With Bob, her husband of 26 years, Phyllis spent many enjoyable weekends biking and exploring the Marin countryside in preparing this book. It was typeset by Phyllis on her personal computer using a desktop publishing program and laser printer. The maps and elevation profiles were made by her as well.

Phyllis is a resident of Penngrove, in Sonoma County, and is the owner of Penngrove Publications.